LITERARY CRITICISM AND CULTURAL THEORY

Edited by

William E. Cain
Professor of English
Wellesley College

T0347652

A ROUTLEDGE SERIES

LITERARY CRITICISM AND CULTURAL THEORY

WILLIAM E. CAIN, *General Editor*

FATAL NEWS

Reading and Information Overload in Early Eighteenth-Century Literature

Katherine E. Ellison

Routledge
Taylor & Francis Group

NEW YORK AND LONDON

Published in 2006 by
Routledge
Taylor & Francis Group
711 Third Avenue,
New York, NY 10017

Published in Great Britain by
Routledge
Taylor & Francis Group
2 Park Square,
Milton Park, Abingdon,
Oxfordshire OX14 4RN

First issued in paperback 2014

Routledge is an imprint of the Taylor and Francis Group, an informa business

© 2006 by Taylor & Francis Group, LLC

ISBN 978-0-415-97626-8 (hbk)
ISBN 978-0-415-86726-9 (pbk)

Library of Congress Cataloging-in-Publication Data

Catalog record is available from the Library of Congress

For Cory and Noah Patterson

Contents

Acknowledgments

The idea for this book, a revision of my dissertation, grew out of an early conversation with Richard Turner about Swift's *A Tale of a Tub;* to him I wish to express my thanks for inspiring my passion for the period. The completion of *Fatal News* also could not have been possible without the guidance of Martine Brownley, John Sitter, and Walter Reed, who read early drafts critically and with great encouragement. Jeff Walker and Laura Otis are to be thanked as well for their helpful suggestions and recommendations for further reading.

I am also indebted to those who have shared their scholarship in the fields of media theory, eighteenth-century literary studies, and the history of science and technology. Conversations at the Folger Shakespeare Library, particularly with fellow participants in the colloquium led by James Bono, "Imagining Nature: Technologies of the Literal and Scientific Revolution," were incredibly helpful as I planned revisions. I am grateful to those who gave me the opportunity to share my ideas publicly as I was working through them, specifically George H. Williams and Sean D. Moore. The DeBartolo Conference for Eighteenth-Century Studies, The Aphra Behn Society, the American Society for Eighteenth-Century Studies, the Northeast Society for Eighteenth-Century Studies, and the Society for the History of Authorship, Reading, and Publishing should also be thanked for giving beginning scholars like myself a forum for learning more directly from others more experienced in the field.

Research was far easier with the help of some excellent library support along the way, at the Folger, at Emory's Woodruff Library, and through the new online collections, *Early English Books Online* and *Eighteenth-Century Collections Online.* All of us owe a great deal to those who have worked long hours to put those databases together.

Just as important have been conversations I have had with students, who always help me see the century from new perspectives. Their surprise observations, disbelieving challenges for proof, and collaborative syntheses of ideas during class discussions have kept me on my toes. Thank you to Emory's Department of English and Emory College for the opportunity to teach eighteenth-century literature and for the time and resources to continue writing.

Introduction

The Idea of Information Overload in the Eighteenth Century

Every age has been an information age. When citizens verbally pass on news, send letters, visit neighbors, or distribute and read written reports of local events, they participate in information systems that order communication and affect the community psychologically, economically, socially, and intellectually. As new technologies develop and old technologies become obsolete, economic models, global relationships, and social attitudes change. What is noteworthy about the late seventeenth and early eighteenth centuries is that the writing of the period reflects the impact of informational change more visibly than previous literatures. By the late seventeenth century information emerges as a concept, and almost immediately it is imagined as a physically and psychologically threatening entity, at once material and immaterial, with the capability of overloading the human body and intellect. Rather than simply record their fear of such a threat, however, authors of the period demonstrate creative methods of information management, critiquing and modifying their information systems by providing alternative models of literacy for the reading public.

Fatal News builds from Benedict Anderson's study of print-capitalism in *Imagined Communities*, specifically from his central argument that "the convergence of capitalism and print technology on the fatal diversity of human language created the possibility of a new form of imagined community, which in its basic morphology set the stage for the modern nation" (46). By isolating part of Anderson's argument to focus on what these "imagined communities" may have looked like during the period, readers can better understand the impact of evolving information systems—of which print is only one technology and of which technology is only one facet—on the early eighteenth-century development of the idea of an imagined collective, a community of seemingly unlike members, perhaps living thousands of miles apart from one another, linked only by a common communication system. Literature of the late seventeenth and early eighteenth centuries stands at a critical—though not necessarily originary—point in the history of global, systematized communication.

By looking closely at the effects of information on the community, the individual citizen, and the text, the literacy models imagined by literary authors of the period can be categorized in three ways. First, authors hypothesize the untapped uses of new communication systems, specifically systems that use secrecy rather than publicity as their means of transmission. Second, they focus on individuals to consider how everyday reading habits must change in order for citizens to better manage the information available. Third, they design narratives that test generic limitations and that demonstrate efficient and inefficient ways of presenting information and, in the cases of John Bunyan, Aphra Behn, Jonathan Swift, and Daniel Defoe, criticize and even satirize textual examples of information mismanagement. In its approach, then, *Fatal News* is more concerned with organizational systems than with technologies. Through readings of exemplary works by these four authors, the study identifies how writers of the period adopt new strategies for managing a perceived increase in the quantity of texts, for understanding readers' roles as producers of texts, and for interpreting texts that must be approached differently because of their delivery. In other words, this study of information focuses on management, interpretation, and consumption as they influence the production of texts in the eighteenth century.[1]

Responding to claims that eighteenth-century communication systems, or contemporary conversations about such systems, forecast the twentieth-century preoccupation with information, I find that the eighteenth-century experience with the proliferation of texts and the expansion of its communication systems is unique in the history of media. Bunyan's *The Pilgrim's Progress* (1678), Behn's *The History of the Nun: or, The Fair Vow-Breaker* (1682), Swift's *A Tale of a Tub* (1704), and Defoe's *A Journal of the Plague Year* (1722) reflect the impact of information on contemporary consciousness. Each challenges historical and theoretical assumptions in media studies about the century as the beginning of today's romance with information and as a transitional point at which citizens shifted away from traditional oral discourses and toward emerging printed discourses. They also challenge Jürgen Habermas's argument that publicity becomes the most effective means of passing on information in the century. Using innovative narrative techniques to illustrate the obstacles and capabilities of rapidly expanding communication networks, these four authors comment on methods of restriction, categorization, and reorganization used by communities to contain and harness the circulation of information. They also foreground the underestimated importance of secrecy in the development of a modern information system.

While the information societies of the eighteenth and twentieth centuries are very different, conversations about them in media studies have been strikingly similar. The eighteenth century possessed none of the inventions that media theorists like Friedrich Kittler find so important in their studies, such as the phonograph, the typewriter, the telegraph, film, and digital media, yet its citizens heard some of the same debates and tropes that recur in contemporary theoretical and popular conversations. This suggests that post-industrial and electronic technologies are not solely responsible for the cultural landscape that has formed around them. As Carla Hesse points out, citizens of both ages demonstrate similar enthusiasm for collaborative authorship, heralded in the eighteenth century by Condorcet and in the twenty-first century by Mikhail Epstein (23–4). Also comparable are visual experiments inspired by new textual technologies, such as the eighteenth-century newspaper, index, and periodical and the twentieth-century web page, as well as discussions about the limitless possibilities of juxtaposing images and text. And though Hesse does not draw the parallel, media theorists have also found similarities between the types of texts that dominate during periods of technological change. New genres emerge that defy definition, such as the novel form and hyperlinked web narratives and, because of the expansion of mass media, scandalous, seditious, politically persuasive, and false information can reach broader audiences (Hesse 25). Indeed, today it is far easier to find (and sometimes impossible to avoid) websites with questionable content than it is to locate an online version of the Declaration of Independence. As Hesse remarks, by the beginning of the nineteenth century "the great texts of the Enlightenment went out of print" (25).

Another discussion that appears often in analyses of eighteenth-century and twentieth-century information societies concerns the promise of universal access. That citizens have the right to be informed is understood, in media theory circles, as a defining characteristic of the Enlightenment. For example, D.N. Rodowick and Tiziana Terranova both subscribe to an idealized notion of information in the eighteenth century. Using Habermas's language, they accept his claim that the public sphere, and the media it depended upon, was a rational and open space of reason. Rodowick calls upon an Enlightenment promise of universal access to information in his analysis of twentieth-century collective action, while Terranova speculates that with today's media citizens have "returned to a pre-Enlightenment mode—that of the spectacle, gossip and manipulation which are seen as undermining reason, rather than being a medium for its expression" (22, 133).[2] As Behn's *History* and Defoe's *Journal* both demonstrate, spectacles and gossip play important roles in the characters' information societies. Behn's protagonist, Isabella de Valerie, is a public spectacle and the subject of town gossip from the moment she leaves her convent to experience the outside world to the final scene when she stands on the scaffold to deliver her execution speech. The infected citizens of Defoe's plague-stricken London become spectacles that the narrator, H.F., watches through his window, and the plague's movement through the city is reported as accurately through gossip as it is in the official Bills of Mortality. In these representative works, spectacle and gossip are not media of the unreasonable but measures against which newer media, like the post and the news report, are tested.

But was the eighteenth century truly the beginning of what became known in the twentieth century as the Age of Information? Though scholars have drawn interesting and often accurate parallels between the cultural effects of print, electronic, and digital information technologies in the two centuries, it is important to question whether it is helpful to make teleological claims that eighteenth-century print culture anticipates how we think of information today. The problem with many media theorists' assumptions about the Restoration and eighteenth centuries is that literature by the most influential creative writers of the century does not provide any evidence of an utopian vision of enlightenment by information. Nor, however, do authors condemn contemporary media out of fear of inevitable apocalypse or assume that the proliferation of texts or the globalization of communication would trap citizens in Doubting Castle rather than lead them to the Celestial City. It is not even so simple as to say that writers like Bunyan, Behn, Swift, and Defoe fit somewhere between enthusiasm and pessimism. What a close analysis of representative works by each author reveals, rather, is an awareness that goes much beyond acceptance or resistance. Each work traces types of adaptation that readers can adopt to deal with the perceived proliferation of texts. Each demonstrates its own process of technological problem solving.

In a footnote, Geoffrey Nunberg writes that "one widely known enthusiast is fond of saying that the analogy of Gutenberg doesn't do the computer justice; what we should really invoke, he says without apparent irony, is the domestication of fire or perhaps the evolution of opposing thumbs" ("Introduction" 20). Nunberg and the unnamed enthusiast may be right. Yet even if the eighteenth-century concept of information does not rival "the evolution of opposing thumbs" in importance, it nonetheless plays a critical role in the evolution of eighteenth-century reading habits, the development of innovative narratives and literary genres, and the construction of new systems and offices of information management. The following chapters thus prove that analogies comparing the effects of Restoration and eighteenth-century communication to those of computer-mediated discourse are not necessary to validate the study of pre-digital information systems.

Readers see in later seventeenth- and eighteenth-century literature a more sustained conversation about media than had ever occurred before. Habermas begins his influential study with this point, describing the late seventeenth- and early eighteenth-century commerce of communication and the way in which the press was a major factor in the emergence of the public sphere: "The great trade cities became at the same time centers for the traffic in news; the organization of this traffic on a *continuous* basis became imperative to the degree to which the exchange of commodities and of securities became continuous" (16). Similarly, Marshall McLuhan sees in the seventeenth and eighteenth centuries crucial periods of adaptation during which "the initial shock gradually dissipates as the entire community absorbs the new habit of perception into all of its areas of work and association" (23).[3] McLuhan calls this period "the real revolution" during which "new model[s] of perception" came into being (23).

While human-centered studies by theorists like McLuhan and Walter Ong focus almost entirely on changes in human consciousness and perception, machine-centered studies of seventeenth- and eighteenth-century communication by historians such as Elizabeth Eisenstein, in contrast, focus primarily on machines and their cultural implications. Until recently, as media theory has grown as a discipline, meetings between the two groups have been rare and, when they have occurred, problematic. For example, Eisenstein, author of the most influential study of seventeenth- and eighteenth-century communication systems to date, attacks McLuhan's approach to the topic in his *The Gutenberg Galaxy* (1962). Most disturbing to Eisenstein is McLuhan's intentional avoidance of historical chronology and what she sees as a suspicious interdisciplinarity that draws from fields as diverse as literature and electromagnetic theory. She wrongly assumes, however, that "to be well versed in modern literary criticism is to be predisposed against chronological narrative regardless of other avant-garde trends" (40). She also focuses only on the structural organization of McLuhan's study and does not comment on whether McLuhan produces any compelling points, perhaps even *because* of his non-linear organization.

The conflict between McLuhan and Eisenstein's approaches to communication in the eighteenth century is symptomatic of a larger tension within media studies between scholars of different academic and professional fields. Studies of print culture and the history of the book, information theory, media studies, and media theory, while seemingly all concerned with the same issues, seem to be separate and unsystematic fields that are rarely in close conversation with one another. Within universities the arts and humanities and social sciences operate without much connection. Within the humanities, eighteenth-century literary scholars often find Eisenstein more helpful than McLuhan, while scholars engaged with theory look more often to recent work by N. Katherine Hayles, Gilles Deleuze, Félix Guattari and others. At the same time, while humanists reference Eisenstein, McLuhan, Martin Heidegger, Deleuze and Guattari, David Bolter, Hayles, and Kittler, for example, social scientists draw more often from Fritz Machlup, Ian Miles, and Daniel Bell.[4] Many universities have already created departments or programs dedicated to the study of information or media, but most promote interdisciplinary work only within the social sciences. Few focus on sharing scientific and humanist perspectives. Discussions also extend outside academe, so that scholars, business professionals, and even political figures speak of similar phenomena yet do so with vastly different terms, methodologies, goals, and textual evidence. While various approaches are of course needed, fields could be learning more from one another.

As a number of twentieth-century historical examinations of eighteenth-century communication show, the most tempting binary of media studies is the pro- or anti-technology argument.[5] In addition to oversimplifying the sophisticated responses that literary authors demonstrate in their writings, such binaries tend to become dated rather quickly, as Nunberg points out when he cites predictions that "photography will kill painting, movies will kill theater, television will kill movies, and so on" ("Introduction" 13). Like any theoretical discipline, media studies has a complicated history and is practiced by scholars with very different—and often contradictory—assumptions about why media are important and how (or whether) conversations about them should enter ongoing dialogues about literature.

Because media theory is relatively new to literary studies, any analysis that bridges the two disciplines will necessarily help define what the field of media studies is and what it is capable of contributing to literary readings. *Fatal News* thus brings together literary, theoretical, and scientific conversations about media that have tended either to be machine-centered or to deny the influence of communication technologies on the eighteenth-century cultural landscape, taking neither side in the debate that sees Eisenstein, as well as Alvin Kernan and Alvin Gouldner, on one side and McLuhan and Ong on the other. Rather, the study takes both views in moderation: print influences cultural practice as well as changes citizens' habits, specifically their reading habits, consciously and unconsciously. What is more interesting, within the context of late-seventeenth and early-eighteenth-century literature, is evidence readers find of experimentation with and revision of alternative systems of organization to better manage information abundance.[6]

THE CONCEPT OF INFORMATION IN THE EIGHTEENTH CENTURY

"Considering how much we ask the word 'information' to do," Nunberg writes, "we don't spend time thinking critically about what it means" ("Farewell" 103). In the twentieth and twenty-first centuries, theorists have struggled to define information and negotiate its meaning in theoretical and popular contexts. In media theory, information is specific to the twentieth century: it is associated with capitalism, consumerism, production, technology, and computers. It is considered one of the three major "revolutions" in history following the agricultural and industrial revolutions.[7] In 1980, for example, as essay collections on information began to appear, Jean-Pierre Dupuy defined an information society as "a phase in the history of capitalism coping with its contradictions" (4). Alistair Duff, who characterizes information in three main ways, allows for broader historical application: in his view information is a workforce, where workers deal with "information in some form" rather than with things, an "explosion" or product for market and technological growth, and abstractly a "spread," or something that "arrives" (16).[8] Similarly, Robert Mitchell and Phillip Thurtle characterize information as warfare, as an economic market, as state-controlled bureaucracy, and as mobile agent between oral and written communication (6).

How can one discuss an eighteenth-century information society, or even an eighteenth-century media state, when such terms did not exist at that time? Certainly, one of the obstacles of writing about information before electronic media is the temptation of imposing a twenty-first-century meaning on a term that in the eighteenth century did not mean what it does today. The term "information society," for instance, did not become popular until the 1960s (Duff 2). Though media theorists disagree on exactly when information emerged as a concept, most look back only so far as the nineteenth century for its origin. Kittler and Terranova, for example, both believe that the "informatization of culture" does not begin until the nineteenth century (Terranova 8). Kittler specifically aligns the origin of the information age with technological invention. Terranova argues that it is not until the nineteenth century that information "is not simply the content of the message" but "also another name for the increasing visibility and importance of such 'massless flows' as they become the *environment* within which contemporary culture unfolds" (8).

The field of linguistics has offered the broadest perspective on the evolution of information as a concept. In a 1986 etymological study, for example, Rafael Capurro finds that in the centuries following the Middle Ages information became an entity to be regarded objectively "as something to be stored and processed" (263). Though he does not specify exactly when that changed occurred, his remarks about Descartes and Leibniz suggest that he locates the change between the seventeenth and eighteenth centuries.[9] Writing in 1996, Orrin E. Klapp also points to the eighteenth century as a fundamental point of definition for the modern Information Age. In his view, the theory of free thinking as developed by Kant reveals that by the eighteenth century "thinking has both a communicative and an informative dimension" (266). Nunberg, a linguist, presents the most persuasive argument about the state of information in the eighteenth century but, like Kittler and Terranova, Nunberg concludes that it is not until the nineteenth century that information can be considered philosophically or abstractly. Nunberg believes that twentieth-century historical considerations of information tend to dramatize the appearance of the term before the nineteenth century in order to justify contemporary enthusiasm about digital technologies. He observes that today's theorists and historians "have to believe [. . .] that the substance that computers traffic in, 'information' in the technical sense of the term, is the same sort of stuff that led to the Reformation and the French Revolution, whether or not contemporaries talked about it in those terms" ("Farewell" 110). Nunberg looks to treatment of the term in other languages and finds that many, such as French, Italian, and modern Greek, retain a plural form that disappeared from English usage in the mid-nineteenth century. In its plural usage, he believes that "informations" even more visibly refers to facts or the materials of instruction. Not coincidentally, it is during the mid-nineteenth century that Nunberg believes the semantic foundation of twentieth-century information begins to form.

Nunberg notes that semantically, information today functions both "particularly" and "abstractly" (110). The particular concerns some "fact, or subject, or event," such as on what day a stage play will be performed, while the abstract sense refers "to a kind of intentional substance present in the world" (110). Nunberg's discussion of abstract information is difficult to follow, because he tends to define the abstract meaning by negation—what abstract information is not—rather than by example. For instance, he explains that information as an abstract term is not connected to the verb "to inform" or anchored in particular speech acts, that it did not appear in English until the mid-nineteenth century, and that it does not refer to the sum of smaller "bits of useful information" (110). Rather, it is what is meant when the twentieth century is referred to as the "Information Age" (110). Nunberg's argument about the difference between eighteenth- and twentieth-century conceptions of information is rooted in this distinction between the particular and the abstract, but he never clarifies exactly how the two are different. He also never explains how the phrase, "Information Age," functions abstractly.

My disagreement with Nunberg concerns his assumption that eighteenth-century authors "had no way [. . .] to speak of information as a kind of abstract stuff present in the world, disconnected from the situations that it is *about*" (111). To prove his point, Nunberg cites a passage in Swift's *Gulliver's Travels* (1726), when Gulliver receives information of "facts" (111). This instance is a safe choice, but other appearances of the term in Swift or in Defoe cannot be so easily classified as particular. In the *Tale*, for example, the narrator writes: "so far preferable is that wisdom which converses about the surface, to that pretended philosophy which enters into the depth of things, and then comes grave back with the informations and discoveries that in the inside they are good for nothing (83). Nunberg would focus only on the fact that the term appears in the plural form, which he argues proves that it refers to facts. Yet what is fascinating about Swift's use of the term is the way it is physically and spatially associated with surface, depth, and meaninglessness. It is this association, I argue, that marks a significant transformation in the meaning of information as ambiguously both material and immaterial. Nunberg's analysis would also discount the verb form of the term in Isabella's cry for help in Behn's *Tale* when she exclaims, "Inform me, oh! Inform me of the nature of that cruel disease, and how thou found'st a cure?" (13). At first glance, Isabella seems to be pleading with her friend Katteriena for facts or instructions about how to recover from a broken heart. Yet, within the context of Isabella's larger communicational dilemma, it becomes increasingly evident as the narrative progresses that she longs to be "informed" in an abstract and general sense. The following chapter on Behn's *History* sets out to prove that Isabella's cry may actually be a defining moment for the period that follows the establishment of the first government postal system.

Though Nunberg's use of literary examples to prove his argument is problematic, his essay and his important anthology *The Future of the Book* (1996) have provided a starting point for twenty-first-century media theorists to think more critically about the importance of information before electronic and digital technologies. Most recently, for example, Mitchell and Thurtle have analyzed the various particular uses of the term during the eighteenth century. While they agree with Nunberg that information in its abstract sense did not emerge until the mid-nineteenth century, they also acknowledge that as "understood particularities of distant knowledge about distant areas, topics, or groups," information "emerged at least as early as the newspaper revolution of the early eighteenth century, and the term became an important part of the political discourse in the late eighteenth century" (6). As evidence, they cite the creation of the Society for Constitutional Information in Britain in 1780 (6).

While it is not necessary to move Nunberg's mid-nineteenth century marker back to the early or late eighteenth century, limiting the meaning of the concept of information to "facts" oversimplifies and even denies late seventeenth- and early eighteenth-century awareness of and response to systems of information management and organization as significant cultural forces. Furthermore, Nunberg's search for and isolation of the term inevitably decontextualizes it. Swift's information may indeed appear to mean only facts or instruction when the sentence is extracted from the work, but if examined within the text's broader considerations of communication, it carries additional semantic baggage. Also important to point out is that the existence of a term in no way validates or prohibits the existence of the concept behind that term. Duff observes that "the prevalence of a belief in the information society does not entail that the information society actually exists in any coherent sense" (15). The opposite is just as true: that citizens of the eighteenth century had not identified themselves as members of an information society does not necessarily mean that they were not part of such a society. Whether or not the word appeared frequently in the literature, it is clear that the eighteenth century was what Susan Crawford would more aptly call an "information-conscious society" (380–5).

Before examining the way in which literary works like *Pilgrim's Progress,* the *History,* the *Tale,* and the *Journal* demonstrate evolving community and individual responses to information, it is first necessary to reconsider what constitutes an "information-conscious society." In her study, Eisenstein, like many after her, interprets the phrase to mean a society dependent upon print. Championing the printing press, she believes that print has been largely ignored as an agent of intellectual and political change, while other possible systems like the postal system have been overemphasized as signs of coming industrialization. Perhaps as a result of her work, however, little attention has been given to the significant role that other information systems, like the post office, played in the development of reading communities linked by common technologies rather than by kinship or geography. For this reason, I define an information-conscious society in a cumulative sense, aware that print, the postal system, espionage, road routes, and other networks all work with and against one another to change the psychological, cultural, and literary consciousness of a community. [10]

Also important in my definition, and discussed only briefly in Eisenstein's and McLuhan's, are oral discourses. Bristol and Marotti, for example, prove that oral messages, printed texts, and manuscripts cannot be thought of simply as separate media. They explain that a text can actually pass back and forth between the three media in the process of production and delivery. Messages, then, do not necessarily exist singularly in oral, manuscript, or print form (6). Bunyan's *Pilgrim's Progress* and Behn's *History* prove Bristol and Marotti's point. Throughout these two narratives, orality and print cannot be easily differentiated as independent media. Interestingly, both Bunyan and Behn address the relationship between oral and written discourses in terms of the postal system rather than print. Bunyan proposes an alternative model of literacy in *Pilgrim's Progress* that unites the local advantages of an oral tradition and the global potential of the postal system, while Behn is interested in the postal system as an integral part of her era's changing economic and political landscape. Her *History* at first seems to prove the incompatibility of the vow, or oral promise, and the post, but by the end both are equally vulnerable to the whims of the public. Isabella's situation also proves that it is an oversimplification to view the relationship between the oral and the printed as progressive of some kind. Though the three "stages" of communication as proposed by Mark Poster—face-to-face and oral, print-mediated, and electronic—are inviting for their clarity and application, narratives like Behn's challenge scholarly attempts to characterize oral discourse as an obsolete antique displaced by the technological triumph of print.

Against Eisenstein's isolation of the printing press, I, like Hesse, argue for a more comprehensive analysis of Reformation and post-Reformation information technologies. In response to Eisenstein, Hesse argues that the canon, the prioritization of the author, and the legal identity of the book as intellectual property did not derive from a single technology but were "the cumulative result of particular social and political choices made by given societies at given moments" (21). [11] Hesse sees Eisenstein's and other historian's and theorist's use of the term "print culture" as the vocabulary of an isolationist perspective, arguing that the term is misleading because it "implicitly carries with it a technological determinism that conflates the history of a means of cultural production (the printing press) with the historical development of a mode of cultural production" (21). Similarly, Ursula K. Heise criticizes Eisenstein on the same issue, pointing out that while it is important to acknowledge the cultural influence that a single technology can have, it is equally important to recognize the effect that the technology has on the "media configuration and its manner of operation as a whole" (157).

INFORMATION AS THREAT: OVERLOAD AND THE EIGHTEENTH-CENTURY READER

Popular and scholarly accounts of information in the twentieth and twenty-first centuries often exclaim the dangers of the current state of communication and characterize information as physically and psychologically destructive, even going so far as to speculate how information will lead to the annihilation of the species.[12] Several of these accounts end with an obvious fear that information will spiral out of control and "explode," destabilizing and overwhelming citizens and nations. David Shenk, for example, writes at the beginning of his study that "when it comes to information, it turns out that one can have too much of a good thing" (15). He describes this condition of excess as "the glut of information" or "data smog" (16). Terranova agrees and believes that twenty-first-century citizens are in fact "overloaded" by information and that this "sheer overload that constitutes contemporary global culture" challenges citizens to "assemble and reinvent a method that [is] able to take in this bewildering variation without being overwhelmed by it" (1). Duff frequently uses terms like "information explosion," "flowing," and "terrifying abundance" (155).[13] Dupuy and Kittler both predict nuclear attack as one inevitable outcome of the uncontrolled global circulation of information. Dupuy also includes terrorism in his list of information-related threats because, in a global information society, nations depend upon others far away and less developed for cheaper products (Dupuy 17). The "explosion" of information has become equated with explosions in a physical sense—nuclear and terrorist bombings in particular.

By the late seventeenth century, readers witnessed a more noticeable distinction between information and knowledge, an opposition that helps explain the portrayal of information as explosive and stifling. Information began to be imagined by authors to be a shallow, one-dimensional, and fluid entity markedly different from knowledge, an image that has persisted through the end of the twentieth century. Swift and Defoe, particularly, address the inherently hierarchical relationship between information and knowledge. Information, as Nunberg supports, is commonly thought of as facts and events, while knowledge is the connection of facts and events to create a general synthesis and understanding. Duff writes, "We say that universities impact knowledge, and would look askance at any university which claimed only to communicate information" (26).[14] The idea of overload is one consequence of the increasingly divergent concepts of information and knowledge during the eighteenth century. Characters are not overloaded by knowledge, but by information. Behn's Isabella, Swift's maddening narrator, and the citizens of Defoe's London break down when they receive messages that they cannot synthesize to create a broader understanding.

Scholars confident in the fact of informational destruction and annihilation would benefit from a reading of Bunyan's *Pilgrim's Progress*, Behn's *History*, Swift's *Tale*, and Defoe's *Journal*, which prove that the fear of information overload is not specific to the post-industrial world. Rather, the idea of information is, and has been at least since the late seventeenth century, inextricably linked to human vulnerability. As Bunyan states in his apology to the first part, the multiplying text that becomes *Pilgrim's Progress* overwhelms him and takes control of the writing process.[15] Sylvia Brown believes that the apology to the first part of *Pilgrim's Progress* goes so far as to describe reading under the duress of textual multiplicity as "a kind of eating up of the reader," as a reading that will eventually "remake the subject" in the image of the text (29). Information in Behn's *History* functions similarly: the protagonist is ambushed by letters and false information in an almost military way, thus causing her to psychologically break down, suffocate one husband, drown another, and finally be decapitated—to go mad and then physically lose her head—in the end. In the *Tale*, Prince Posterity is unable to keep up with the number of pamphlets being posted and torn down before he can read them all. Swift's narrator, for whom information is a crowd that squeezes the individual, repeatedly represents information as a suffocating and evasive presence that will potentially turn citizens inside out, making them surfaces without depth. Information in Defoe's *Journal* is as infectious as the plague. The citizens of H.F.'s London receive so much information about the virus's apparent movement that it directs their behavior and in the end endangers them. In these works information consumes, corners, floods, explodes, and strangles. It is cannibalistic, destructive, and always hyperbolic. Perhaps most importantly, information takes over characters' bodies, transforming them into one-dimensional texts.

So how could citizens be afraid of a concept that scholars like Nunberg argue did not even begin to emerge until the nineteenth century? As Bunyan, Behn, Swift, and Defoe prove, citizens undoubtedly noticed textual proliferation and expanding communication networks and changed their attitudes toward reading, problem solving the challenges of information before the term itself was widely used. That the term "information" or its verb form "to inform" appear only in key passages in the works following *Pilgrim's Progress* is itself significant: struggling to find a word or expression for the characters' vulnerabilities, Behn, Swift, and Defoe all come upon the term during moments of narrative crisis.

Surprising to today's media theorists would be the fact that citizens as early as the late seventeenth and early eighteenth centuries were consciously problem solving ways to avoid feeling overloaded. Twentieth- and twenty-first-century media theorists would seem to be merely repeating the cry of Swift's narrator and agreeing that meaningful experience and true knowledge will somehow be drowned out by the meaningless and superficial noise caused by the proliferation of mass media. Yet authors like Behn, Swift, and Defoe not only recognized the threat of information but went a step further to question, first, whether bodies and minds could indeed be overwhelmed by information and, second, whether citizen fear of overload could be harnessed to invent more creative and efficient organizational systems. Their conclusions much resemble what theorists today would call a realization of the virtual. In his groundbreaking study of the virtual, Pierre Lèvy explains virtuality in terms of texts, bodies, and economies. Textually, Lèvy argues that when news of an event is publicly delivered, the event is lifted out of the original spatial and temporal frames, or deterritorialized. This information, in turn, is "at the same time [the event's] prolongation" (74). As information is transmitted to one receiver after another, he finds, the event takes place again and again, always in a different time and place. This "actualization," as Lèvy calls it, results in yet more messages, so that the first transmission of messages itself becomes an event that can be reported. "Events and information about events," Lèvy summarizes, "exchange their identities and functions at each stage of the dialectic of signifying processes" (75). In his analysis, Lèvy often depends upon terms like "deterritorialization" and "framing" to describe the actualization of an event as news story. Rodowick also uses the term, stating that "the consolidation and expansion of the media state as a virtual information 'territory' in conjunction with the actual transnational movements of people is producing what might be called a cosmopolitan public sphere" (13). Readers see this most clearly in Defoe's *Journal*. In H.F.'s account, boundaries are drawn and crossed in the most local of all spaces—the human body, for example—as well as in some of the most global—the trade routes and boundaries of a world newly engaged in seemingly boundless exchange.

Lèvy's discussion of the virtualization of bodies provides a helpful framework for analyzing the language Restoration and eighteenth-century writers use to critique information. In their writings, information is often described as a material entity that can either damage or protect human bodies. While Christian is physically at risk on his journey and his safety depends upon his ability to apply the lessons of scripture, Christiana's body is never truly in danger. In fact, critics of the second part of *Pilgrim's Progress* have complained that her journey does not have the impact of Christian's *because* she is never physically threatened. What I see happening by the second part, however, is the virtualization of Christiana's body: because she has information about events—what happened to Christian on his journey—she is able to avoid even the risk of harm. This allows readers to recognize that her adventure is not a copy or mere repetition of her husband's but an actualization of it. Her pilgrimage is a reinforcement of faith in the improbable. As Lèvy would describe, the information Christiana receives inspires her to create her own media event, which is then communicated to others who, in turn, cross the river themselves. That she is accompanied by a large crowd by the end of the journey is not surprising; it is perhaps more surprising that *Pilgrim's Progress* has only two parts, since readers know that the event will "take place again and again" (Lèvy 74). Similarly, it is the female body that undergoes a virtual conversion in Behn's *History*, so that by the end Isabella has transformed herself into a letter. She becomes the medium that once trapped her. Information in Swift's *Tale* makes bodies, male or female, malleable, impressionable, and even reversible. The *Journal* records the anxiety of a population that suddenly can neither understand nor control the boundaries of their bodies or their city, and as the invisible virus permeates one body's tissues after another the town establishes policies that attempt to build literal, physical boundaries between the infected and the healthy, citizens and strangers.

Terranova believes that information is "immaterial only" until the twenty-first century and becomes materialized only because of the theoretical use of physical concepts, such as entropy, noise, and nonlinearity, to describe it, yet a cursory glance at these works reveal that the idea of information as material and thus physically threatening goes back at least as far as the Restoration, and probably further. In Swift's *Tale* and Defoe's *Journal*, readers find two very different treatments of information as a material and visceral entity. In the *Tale*, the narrator often describes bodies dissected and turned inside out, along with physiological behaviors, such as belching, defecating, and blowing, that involve the movement of information through the body. The text of the *Tale*, with its excessive introductory matter and marginalia, lists of metaphors, and visible defects, exteriorizes its reading and revision process. In contrast, Defoe's *Journal* depicts bodies tortured by an invisible contaminant that H.F. likens to infectious information. London citizens know that the infection somehow enters their bodies, but they cannot force it out any more successfully than the Bills of Mortality can report it.

Mitchell and Thurtle characterize past distinctions between information and bodies when they observe that "information, so the story goes, exists between elements, whereas bodies are the elements themselves" and that "information, in short, operates through the metaphysics of absence, whereas bodies depend on the metaphysics of space" (1). Introducing a new subfield of media theory that they call "materialistic information studies," they work across academic disciplines to examine information as a creative process of alternating embodiment and disembodiment (2). Information creates new possible "fleshy experience[s]," which readers may see most dramatically in *Pilgrim's Progress,* such as when Christiana's postal correspondence with God signals the beginning of the virtual experience of pilgrimage (3). That her journey marks her disembodiment is evidenced by her conversation with her neighbors, when acts such as crossing a river require both physical and metaphorical readings. Her pilgrimage is virtual in that it represents an alternative reality, much like the dream state of the narrator, when time and space are transformed and Christiana, freed from the limitations of her life in the City of Destruction, can work through her problems (Lèvy 74). *Pilgrim's Progress,* as a whole, moves from the embodied to the disembodied, and arrival at the Celestial City completes the ultimate transformation.

It is important to note that the tension between human bodies and information may be part of a larger trend in literary language of the seventeenth and eighteenth centuries. Douglas Bruster, for example, identifies a late-Elizabethan genre he calls "embodied writing," in which authors begin to describe the body with more detail than before and in which characters are given a "bodily presence" (50). He notes that embodied writing "tended to collapse the traditional distance between bodies and texts, and in doing so brought about important changes in the cultural status of print" (51). One must also remember the connection between the dissected body and the Renaissance satirical tradition that W. Scott Blanchard identifies, in which the Renaissance satirist "wishes to be true to the medical pedigree of the term 'anatomy'" and "presumably wishes to dissect his subject—the world of learning and of intellectuals—until the etiology or pathology of its illness has been determined" (60). That information, particularly when conceived of textually, will by the mid-eighteenth century begin to be described in terms of the body, may not be surprising.

There are a number of ways one might focus a study of information in the late seventeenth and early eighteenth centuries: for example, by examining economies, technological developments, ethical issues, or social problems. An area of information and media studies that has not received as much attention and that literary texts of the period can help readers better understand, however, is the emergence of the concept of information as a cultural force. Reflecting contemporary worries about interpretation and reading in an age in which printed materials, letters, and even oral messages travel faster and in greater numbers than ever before, works by seventeenth- and eighteenth-century authors remind us that the idea of information overload did not emerge suddenly when the first computers went on sale. Though authors of the time were only beginning to use the term, their characters react to the perceived dangers of information and demonstrate possible solutions for managing it. Bunyan, Behn, Swift, and Defoe's works show readers the constructive, rather than destructive, potential of information.

Chapter One

Information *ad infinitum:* Bunyan's Lessons in Careful Reading in *The Pilgrim's Progress*

Whether or not Christiana's journey in the second part of *Pilgrim's Progress* represents a continuation of the concerns of her husband's pilgrimage or an entirely new narrative with little connection to the first part has been a repeated question in Bunyan scholarship of the past three decades. Studies of the 1970s, like Stanley Fish's consideration of memory, interpretation, and what he sees to be the work's "antiprogressive" pattern, rarely mention Christiana except in passing (229). Roger Sharrock's mid-seventies study highlights the differences between the two parts, defending and yet simplifying the artistic merit of Christiana's story when he writes that "it presents a cheerful, teeming picture of the life of a seventeenth-century godly family and of the small separatist community made up of a few such families" ("Women and Children" 175). Writing at the same time, R.M. Frye believes that the second part promotes the proper relation of the individual to the community and the Church (145). Frye's focus on community has come to dominate scholarship of Christiana's journey. More recently, for example, Michael Davies reiterates Frye's claim that Christiana's journey is a "corporate, cooperative, and collective mission" (327). Nick De Marco agrees and goes a step further to announce that the second part is a disturbing portrait of "the total passivity of the individual in a communal context," repeating Ronald Knox's now famous description of Christiana's pilgrimage as a "walking tour" and David Daiches's assessment of it as "a tourist's visit" (De Marco 47, Knox 206, Daiches 588).

By the 1980s, scholars such as N.H. Keeble and U. Milo Kaufmann pay closer attention to the second part on its own terms.[1] Keeble counters the general opinion that "their association appears as a mere circumstance, an accident of biography," while Kaufmann wonders if Christiana's story represents less a "mellowing" on Bunyan's part and more accurately the author's reconsideration of "the balance between opprobrium and approval as they are displayed toward fellow Christians" (Keeble 3, Kaufmann 180). More recent critiques take issue with previous scholars' avoidance of gender discussions. Richard L. Greaves, for example, warns readers not to assume that the second part represents Bunyan's support of gender equality simply because it follows a female protagonist to the Celestial City. Building from Frye and other scholarship that establishes the community focus of the second part, Kathleen Swaim discusses the work's later concern with communal responsibility and gender, concluding that "scriptural and spiritual evidence predominates in the masculine part I; material culture, social organization, and nurturance claim priority for the feminine part II" (4). My interest in Christiana's journey is not at odds with early or recent scholarship, but I find Swaim's comments on the relative sociability of the second part to be most in line with broader changes in the information systems of the late seventeenth century.

Though *Pilgrim's Progress* predates the industrial era by well over a century, it nonetheless engages in a critical examination of the impact of communication technologies, specifically print and postal system, on everyday citizens like the narrator. Grant Holly goes so far as to conclude that Bunyan's most celebrated work is the "product of a rigorous technological order—of engraving, mechanical reproduction, book production" (150). Sharrock agrees with Holly and believes that *Pilgrim's Progress* "marks an important staging-post in the transition from an oral to a print culture, " but he does not outline exactly how that transition is represented ("When at the first" 74). My reading of *Pilgrim's Progress* participates in three main conversations about the text, beginning first with observations like Sharrock's and Holly's that Bunyan's work is a unique product of print technology. Second, I build from and complicate arguments that Christiana's part is mainly— some would even say solely—about community and public worship and, third, I reconsider what and how the allegory teaches readers about new interpretive practices, arguing in the end that *Pilgrim's Progress* highlights conflicts already present in communities facing a technological transition, during which communication systems contributed to increasingly diverse literacy levels and reading habits among neighbors living and working together.

A comparison of Christian and Christiana's departures, interactions with neighbors, and different experiences on the path to the Celestial City proves that as the relationship between speech and writing, script and print, changed, so too did local relationships between neighbors linked by region, ethnicity, and kinship, and globally between citizens far distant from one another geographically and socially. Like Isabel Hofmeyr, who wonders why despite international popularity the author and his work are still valued in academic circles solely for their "Englishness," I take into consideration Bunyan and *Pilgrim's Progress* as global phenomena (2). Readers in the work who understand texts and use communication technologies in similar ways, whether miles or nations apart, form a globally-connected network that much resembles what Anderson calls an imagined community, a virtual group united by a growing information system.[2]

Studied together and not separately, as has been the approach of many Bunyan scholars, the two parts of *Pilgrim's Progress* represent different perspectives within a larger metaphor for reading and textual sharing. In the end, the couple's two journeys prove that modern communication technologies, of which print and the postal system are two examples, need not be at odds with one another or with script and traditional oral discourses. The dichotomy that McLuhan and Ong believe to have existed between print and speech during the late seventeenth century is supported during Christian's journey but challenged by Christiana's. Neither a warning against the dangers of print and the developing postal system nor an enthusiastic nod toward those technologies, Bunyan's work brings to the foreground the potential consequences, positive and negative, of the gradual technological shift from script, a term Ong and Eisenstein reserve for oral utterance, to print (Ong 84). In her groundbreaking study of early modern print culture, Eisenstein wonders if "[p]erhaps this phenomenon might become somewhat less elusive if the relationship between communications systems and community structures was more carefully explained" (131). Bunyan may well have been presenting the same challenge to his contemporaries by subtly addressing the effects of new communication technologies on the communities that live along Christian's path. On Christiana's journey, readers learn that women occupy unique roles in their information system as readers and interpreters.[3]

In contrast to communities like H.F.'s London in *A Journal of the Plague Year*, which hear about the approaching plague from visitors and read about its path in the weekly Bills of Mortality, Christian's town never receives public warning of its future disaster. H.F.'s neighbors, regardless of their spiritual or moral bearing, have access to widely-circulated reports of approaching disaster, but in *Pilgrim's Progress* it is Christian alone to whom the secret of the city's fate is disclosed. A solitary informant, Christian knows that "our City will be burned with fire from Heaven, in which fearful overthrow, both my self, with thee, my Wife, and you my sweet babes, shall miserably come to ruine" (8).

Significantly, this prophecy does not come from a heavenly messenger, nor does Christian experience a jarring vision of future destruction; rather, he draws his own conclusion based on his reading of scripture. For him, the book "inform[s]" him of his community's future and is a thing, an object "made by him that cannot lye" (8, 11). In line with Ong's observations of early print culture, Christian's attitude toward the Bible, which he significantly calls "a Book" and not scripture, supports the claim that "[o]nce print has been fairly well interiorized, a book was sensed as a kind of object which 'contained' information, scientific, fictional or other, rather than, as earlier, a recorded utterance" (Ong 126).[4] Ong further argues that a "script" represents an utterance, while writing and the book represent "a coded system of visible marks" (84). Christian certainly views his book as a system of codes to be deciphered during reading, but he also interprets its words as inevitable events, which complicates Ong's assumptions about the written word as object: "The alphabet implies [. . .] that a word is a thing, not an event" (91). For Christian, the Word becomes an event during interpretation, so that reading is as much an act of creation as writing is.[5] Davies believes that the distress Christian suffers during and after he interprets scripture supports the contemporary reader's fear that reading is a difficult and even agonizing practice, so that Christian's burden represents the burdens of reading (3).

Christiana's decision to travel to the Celestial City is not prompted by her interpretation of the book. Instead, she is visited by a divine messenger who gives her specific information both verbally and in writing, a moment that evokes earlier oral traditions at the same time that it marks the first postal delivery in *Pilgrim's Progress*. "[O]pportunely I had a Dream of the well-being of my Husband, and a Letter sent me by the King of that Country where my Husband dwells" she explains, and "[t]he Dream and the Letter together so wrought upon my mind, that they forced me to this way" (169). Hofmeyr notes that *Pilgrim's Progress* comes from a tradition that imagines a "public sphere that straddled heaven and earth" (26). "In this divine order," she continues, "texts circulated between this world and the next and in some instances, were produced in heaven and made their way to earth" (26). This is particularly true in the second part. Christian's community is not in direct written contact with the heavens; he can only read his book and draw his own conclusions. Christiana's community, however, maintains an open connection with "the King of that Country" through post and courier and learns of heavenly news events through public reports that seem to travel with lightning speed (169).

By the time Christiana receives her letter from God, the way to heaven is a matter of public record. Right away in the second book, readers learn from Mr. Sagacity that Christian's entire journey has somehow been transcribed, published, and archived in the town records. "[T]here are but few Houses that have heard of him and his doings," Sagacity mentions, "but have sought after and got the *Records* of his Pilgrimage" (144). While in the first part the community refuses to read Christian's book to confirm his interpretation, in the second they are avid readers, searching for records as soon as they hear about Christian's adventures. Though uninterested in and suspicious of scripture, they seek out public records with great interest. In the time between the first and second pilgrimages, the postal system, print technology, and public archive are efficient enough that Christiana can rely upon them, as well as on verbal information, for a safe journey.[6]

If Christiana's story is a "cheerful, teeming picture of the life of a seventeenth-century godly family and of the small separatist community made up of a few such families" as Sharrock believes, it is so because of the ease with which the families of the second part can communicate with one another over great distances ("Women and Children" 175). Charles II's Act of 1660, often referred to as the Post Office Charter, established a legal precedent for the postal system and would be followed by several laws that attempted to regulate the distribution of mail (Robinson 48).[7] From the Act of 1660 on, regulation became the key goal of the government, and "for better or for worse, [it] assumed the responsibility for improving the means of communication, though its arrangements usually lagged far behind the public demand" (77). Late seventeenth-century delivery routes, which were largely organized on a wheel pattern in which six rural branches extended out from the central London Office, supported both official and private mail correspondences. One problem with the pattern, however, was that nearby towns that happened to fall on different mail routes could not communicate with one another cheaply because the postage rate was determined by the mileage traveled and not the actual distance between destinations. Mail to neighboring towns was not direct but traveled first to the London office and then back out again. The postal system changed the pattern of correspondence in the English countryside—a change reflected on the road to the Celestial City.

Christian seeks out deliverance, but Christiana waits for it to come to her—and it does. Both her invitation to pilgrimage and her later invitation to enter the Celestial City are by letter, mailed from the most central of offices and delivered to her doorstep.[8] When she receives her letter from God, Christiana suddenly realizes that her husband is accessible to her if she is willing to cut all ties with her current society and join his, a society with the most efficient global information technologies available and a society capable of instantaneous and simultaneous communication between members. [9] Davies believes Christiana's wish to join her husband is motivated by guilt, since in the first part she fails to fulfill her domestic duty to honor and follow her husband (337). Margaret Soenser Breen agrees and sees Christiana's journey as a departure from her self and as a sign of her complete subordination to her husband (337).[10] Certainly, Christiana feels guilty and wants to reunite with her husband, but within the context of this study it is important to note that their meeting is possible only because their two communities are able to communicate with one another. That the medium of communication is the post, when communication could have been established by any other number of methods, suggests that the information systems of both the City of Destruction and the Celestial City have changed between the first and second parts.

Once in direct contact with the "King of that Country," Christiana is no longer able to communicate with those closest to her (169). As she prepares for pilgrimage with her children, for example, she is unexpectedly visited by two neighbor women:

> But while they were thus about to be gon, two of the Women that were Christiana's Neighbours, came up to her House and knocked at her Dore. To whom she said as before. *If you come in Gods Name, come in.* At this the Women were stun'd, for this kind of Language they used not to hear, or to perceive to drop from the Lips of Christiana. (149)

The women's dialogue reveals that a linguistic split has occurred. Christiana speaks in the allegorical language of the Celestial City, but the women perceive her as mad like her husband in the first part. [11] Christiana says she will "go after my good Husband," but what the women hear is that she has lost her mind and is about to commit suicide. "[P]ray for your poor Childrens sake, do not so unwomanly cast away your self," they respond with obvious shock at Christiana's turn of mind. Phrases that in the first part were considered only allegorically, such as "over the River," now take on the physical meaning of drowning, so that the two interpretations of the phrase alienate one another and render communication between the women impossible (130).[12]

Eisenstein wonders why most historians assume that print, and I would include other information technologies like the postal system as well, necessarily unified communities and made possible the expansion of Protestantism, pointing out the possibility that the opposite may be just as accurate. That print and other information technologies may have "contributed to dividing Christendom before spreading Protestantism are possibilities that have gone unexplained" (Eisenstein 29). "In accounts of the Reformation as in accounts of other movements," she finds, "the effects produced by printing tend to be drastically curtailed and restricted to the single function of 'spreading' ideas" (28). The effect of modern communication systems on Christiana's community, in the early scenes of the narrative, is characterized more by division than unification. Opened channels of global correspondence result in the interruption of local correspondence, which parallels conflicts inherent in the early British postal system. New access to global correspondence, coupled with the breakdown of local communication networks, also reveals that seventeenth-century information systems are both expanding in geographical reach yet shrinking on the local level. [13]

To address the problems experienced by small rural communities with little or no access to inconvenient and expensive postal routes, branch roads and byposts were created. "These additions," Robinson finds, "were tending to make the ill-shaped wheel of the main post roads into a web of routes that would in time gossamer the whole land" (65).[14] "Almost simultaneously with the origin of stock markets," Habermas confirms, "postal services and the press institutionalized regular contacts and regular communication" (16). Route expansion occurred very slowly, however, and many towns and residents remained disconnected and alienated from the information society growing around them. Habermas sees this alienation as partly intentional, because merchants preferred communicating with one another without the interference of frequent neighborhood stops and also liked to keep their business affairs private. Also, government officials used print and the postal system only for administrative purposes and wanted to monitor closely all information that changed hands (16). As Habermas concludes, "[n]either had a stake in information that was public" (16).

The degree of publicity of information, whether apocalyptic prophecy or the main character's private emotions, marks an important distinction between the beginnings of the first and second parts of *Pilgrim's Progress*. Though he attempts to pass the information to others so that they, too, can be saved, Christian's neighbors resist his message and prevent it from becoming a public announcement that could save the town from destruction.[15] His affinity for reading does not conflict with the community's norms when he keeps his interpretations to himself, but when he attempts to share the prophecy with others he upsets his family and neighbors, is shunned by the community and presumed to be insane, and finally is forced to leave the town. Habermas also describes the same kind of incompatibility that Bunyan portrays between the town's accepted modes of correspondence and the news Christian tries to introduce into the public sphere. He claims that "[t]he new sector in communications, with its institutions for a traffic in news, fitted in with the existing forms of communication without difficulty as long as the decisive element—publicness—was lacking" (16). The beginning of the second part demonstrates this incompatibility once again, since Christiana receives private, not public, verbal and written messages from God. Further, her message is of personal and not public consequence, because her correspondence merely confirms for her that her husband is in the Celestial City and that she is currently on a sinful path that will prevent her from ever joining him. By the end of their journeys, however, Christian will still keep his message for himself alone even though it could help the community, and Christiana will become the center of a large community of pilgrims even though her message was intended only for her. The private message leads to the formation of a new community, while the public one alienates the lone interpreter.

While in the beginning of the first part Christian is forced, against his will, to keep the prophecy to himself, which represents the failure of public correspondence, in the second part secrecy signals successful communication. Though he must become a repository of the secret, Christian's town prevents him from administering the information in a way that would save them from future destruction.[16] In this way, then, the first part demonstrates not the deliberate withholding of information but the reverse: the surprising refusal of a community to show any interest whatsoever in a secret that is offered to them. Christian's is a city that revels in not knowing.[17] The second part, however, begins with the appearance of a courier named Secret, so that the transmission of information between the two cities is aligned with secrecy. God's personal secretary, Secret passes on only that information needed to motivate Christiana to leave the City of Destruction. During his visit, Secret keeps information from overwhelming her, noticing her trembling and introducing himself in a way that abates her fear. He tells her his name, that he visits on behalf of "those that are high," and that he visits because he has heard a "report" that she is feeling guilty about her past treatment of her husband. Then he informs her that she is invited to join Christian in the Celestial City (147). Next, he provides evidence of his verbal invitation by giving her a letter written by God. What he shares is arguably not a secret: the narrator has already stated that Christian's journey and fate are matters of public record. Part of an organized office whose job is to sort and present information in a strategic, organized way, Secret represents the first conscious systematization of information, solving the problem of publicity of the first part by emphasizing the secret *nature* of that information whether it is truly a secret or not. Eisenstein would not be surprised by this pattern, because she finds that during the early print era "[t]he notion that valuable data could be preserved best by being made public, rather than by being kept secret, ran counter to tradition, led to clashes with new censors, and was central both to early-modern science and to Enlightenment thought" (116). The first part of *Pilgrim's Progress* captures this suspicion of public information, here information printed in the Bible and accessible to those who are literate, and the beginning of the second part offers secrecy as a possible solution for the communication breakdown that occurs when the community is not yet ready for the prophecy to be publicized. Not until the last half of the second part will publicity surpass secrecy as the most effective way of passing on information.

Secret's visit suggests that the late seventeenth-century public sphere, as Habermas conceives of it and Bunyan represents it in his allegory, must develop a rhetoric of privacy in order to publicize information successfully. Throughout the first scenes of the second part, characters are motivated to action by private messages, not public ones, and as a result Christiana is joined by numerous pilgrims along the way to the Celestial City. Uninterested in reading her husband's book, Christiana is persuaded to go on pilgrimage after she receives the letter and witnesses the opening of "a broad Parchment [. . .] in which were recorded the sum of her ways" (146). Unlike Christian, who interprets a prophecy in a text meant to be read by all, Christiana reads a *personal* history of her past sins, a history meant only for her. The biography, anonymously authored and mysteriously delivered, opens communication between the grieving widow and a network of readers and writers that includes her deceased husband. Though citizens have access to public town records and the Bible, which build collective remembrance, highly personalized texts addressed to individuals provide the foundation for the second journey.

Secret's discriminating disclosure of information about Christiana's future parallels the narrator's goals for the second part of *Pilgrim's Progress*. For those readers unable to discover the hidden meanings of Christian's journey—who felt as though they were missing important information—the author offers this second story of the grieving wife, whose journey will unlock the secrets of the pilgrim's progress from the City of Destruction to the Celestial City:

> Besides, what my first Pilgrim left conceal'd,
> Thou my brave Second Pilgrim hast reveal'd;
> What Christian left lock't up and went his way
> Sweet Christiana opens with her Key. (139)

Though Christiana's scene of departure emphasizes secrecy, the author stresses that the second part, as a whole, is designed to disclose the secrets of the first part.[18] Christian does not intentionally leave the meaning of his journey "lock't up" but rather is forced to keep his secret because of his community's disinterest; similarly, the narrator fears that he has also failed to communicate his message to his community of readers. Like Secret, the narrator prefaces the writing that will follow with a personal address to the readers, explaining to them what they are about to experience. Readers may expect meanings to be easily decipherable, just as the pilgrims of the second part expect important information about the way to the Celestial City to be easily and quickly available.

From Christian's initial interpretation of the Bible's prophecy to the appearance of God's courier before Christiana's departure, written texts divide the community of the City of Destruction. Reading in the first part and the beginning of the second, in fact, isolates the main characters from their neighbors, who avoid reading as much as they avoid learning the secret of Christian's revelation. As soon as Christian leaves the City of Destruction, there is the sense that others would believe the prophecies if only they would "read of them" for themselves, but Christian remains the sole character in the first part who reads (11).[19] When Obstinate and Pliable question him, Christian cites examples from the Bible of the advantages of leaving the city, and he explains that "the Governour of that Countrey, hath Recorded that in this Book," likening scripture to a public record that documents future events as well as past ones (12). When Christian offers it to Obstinate, telling him to "[r]ead it so, if you will, in my Book," Obstinate responds as if offended: "*Tush*, said Obstinate, *away with your Book; will you go back with us, or no?*" (10). Pliable, who accompanies Christian for a short while, also avoids reading each time a book is offered to him. Pliable asks several questions about the prophecy and about what to expect in the Celestial City, and at first Christian insists that the answers are "in my Book," suggesting that Pliable should read it (11). Pliable subtly persuades Christian to paraphrase the book for him.

Pliable's dialogue emphasizes his need for oral, not written, responses, while Christian's responses highlight sight and reading. "Well said," Pliable repeats several times, remarking that "[t]he hearing of this is enough to ravish ones heart" and that he is glad "to hear of these things" (12). Christian, in contrast, speaks repeatedly of eyes, seeing, and words, explaining to Pliable that they will meet "Creatures that will dazle your eyes to look on them" and "see Men that by the World were cut in pieces" (12). "I can better conceive of them with my Mind," Christian admits, "then speak of them with my

Tongue: But yet since you are desirous to know, I will read of them in my Book" (11). Pliable and Obstinate's reactions can be interpreted in two ways: on one hand, their reactions are symptomatic of their spiritual doubt and lack of faith in God's words and works. On the other hand, their reactions indicate that they may in fact be unable to read Christian's book for themselves, avoiding his offers to look at the book because they wish to keep their illiteracy a secret. Pliable forces Christian to deliver his interpretation of the Bible orally, as if he is giving a sermon.

Christian's book becomes a source of shame for the wayward characters he meets during his journey, who refer to the book as a sign of insanity, not salvation. When Christian admits that he gained all of his current information by "reading this Book in my hand," Worldly-Wiseman exclaims that reading is "meddling" and results in nothing but "fall[ing] into thy distractions, which distractions do not only unman men (as I perceive has done thee) but they run them upon desperate ventures, to obtain they know not what" (16). Worldly-Wiseman, then, equates reading with snooping. From his perspective, books contain secrets that readers should not disclose. Disclosure of those secrets, he explains, causes readers to go mad, as if the information revealed is too overwhelming for the human psyche to handle.

As he advises Christian, Worldly-Wiseman argues for verbal communication over written communication and reveals that Christian's difficult journey to the Celestial City is in part a metaphor for the act of reading. Worldly-Wiseman urges Christian to avoid "the dangers that thou in this way wilt run thyself into," and Christian adapts the language of disclosure and asks him to "Pray sir open this secret to me" (16). The secret Worldly-Wiseman reveals is really no secret at all, as readers learn when Evangelist later scolds Christian for walking off the path. Worldly-Wiseman claims that a visit to the Village of Morality will ease his burden, where he will meet Legality or his son Civility, who "can do it (to speak on) as well as the old Gentleman himself" (16). Faced with a critical decision, Christian gives in to Worldly-Wiseman's counsel, choosing a talking cure—speaking on—over the book he holds in his hand.

Reviving the New Testament emphasis on reading and listening as unique sensory activities that, together, keep the faithful in touch with God, *Pilgrim's Progress* restates the cooperative relationship between orality and print within the contemporary context of technological development. In the Book of Revelation in particular, which is central to Bunyan's narrative, reading and listening are described as complementing one another: "Blessed is he that readeth, and they that hear the words of this prophecy" (Rev. 1.3). By the late seventeenth century, however, more efficient printing methods, a relatively new system of mail correspondence regulated by the government, and increased literacy complicated communication between citizens within close communities. Eisenstein finds that "[m]embers of the same reading public, who confronted the same innovation in the same region at the same time, were nonetheless affected by it in markedly different ways" (130). "The displacement of pulpit by press is significant not only in connection with secularization," she continues, "but also because it points to an explanation for the weakening of local community ties" (131). Even though citizens still attended church services together to listen to sermons, not every member of the congregation could necessarily read transcriptions of the sermons or translations of scripture once they arrived home (Eisenstein 129).

The cornerstone of McLuhan's theory, though not directly applicable to *Pilgrim's Progress,* nonetheless raises helpful questions about the relationship between communication and community that interest Eisenstein. "Those who experience the first onset of a new technology," he writes, "respond most emphatically because the new sense ratios set up at once by the technological dilation of eye or ear, present men with a surprising new world, which evokes a vigorous new 'closure,' or novel pattern of interplay among all the senses together" (22–23). It is impossible to prove that Bunyan's allegory demonstrates an "interplay among all the senses" that is attributable entirely to technology or that such an interplay is not present in pre-print texts, but both parts of *Pilgrim's Progress* present oral and written communication, whether by sermon, verbal lesson, print, post, or emblem, alongside one another, testing each against the other. Hofmeyr believes that Bunyan turns the tables and presents print as a "traditional" rather than a new technology, so that the implication is that characters need not "adjust" to print because "technologies of modernity, in this case print and literacy, are likewise made ancestral" (26). What I find, however, is that Bunyan does not deny that print and the postal system are communication technologies that present new and unprecedented challenges to citizens. Rather, he revitalizes oral discourse and reminds readers of the importance of the verbal, of the interdependent relationship that has always existed between the oral and the written, and of the teachings of scripture. Scripture, he emphasizes, has always been about discovering new ways of seeing *and* hearing, about suddenly gaining access to the meanings of sights and sounds that were always present but not intelligible until the witness or listener found true faith in God. In this way, *Pilgrim's Progress* does not antiquate print: it modernizes the oral and makes both media relevant for the contemporary believer.

The "real revolution," McLuhan concludes, "is in this later and prolonged phase of adjustment of all personal and social life to the new model of perception set up by the new technology" (23). *Pilgrim's Progress,* itself divided into two parts that represent the mindsets of two different decades within a quickly changing technological environment, illustrates the "absorption" and "adjustment" to which McLuhan refers. At the same time, it portrays the "new habit of perception" as both a technological and a *spiritual* process, adopting scripture's negotiation of the oral and the written to prove that new media need not divide communities. Even Bunyan's choice to mimic vernacular speech in his writing is an attempt to unite the two modes of discourse. Further, while the first part presents a clear distinction between the spoken and the written that illustrates Eisenstein's point about community division rooted in literacy and religious conflict, the second part offers a solution for the disunity. Though literate like her husband, Christiana does not insist that Mercie and Timorous read her letter for themselves. As Maxine Hancock finds, it is likely that Mercie is in fact unable to read just as Pliable and Obstinate are, though unlike them she wishes to become a reader during her journey (87). In answer to the neighbors' questions about her change of mind, Christiana first explains her depression, recounts the events of the previous night, and then pulls out her letter and reads it *to* them.[20] Only when they are privy to the language of the letter do the women understand Christiana's way of speaking. Through this scene, Bunyan emphasizes that the communication breakdown is not about being literate or illiterate but about flexibility. The issue is not whether Mercie and Timorous are literate but whether Christiana can find a way to communicate her meaning to them and they are able to adapt to the metaphorical language that she adopts once she is in communication with God. Timorous may not agree with Christiana and Mercie's decisions to journey to the Celestial City, but unlike Obstinate and Pliable, she understands where and why they are going.

The first step to more effective communication in the second part of *Pilgrim's Progress* is the efficient administration of secrecy, and the second step is to learn that literacy is not an either/or ability. Both Christian and Christiana reach the Celestial City because they develop their literacy during their journeys. It becomes clear after Christian's visit to the Interpreter's house, for example, that reading is not simply the ability to understand words on a page but also the ability to translate metaphor into useful everyday knowledge. Christiana's encounter with the Interpreter takes readers a step further to consider the unique challenges facing an experienced reader. Even though Christian deciphers the hidden message of his city's imminent destruction and joins a discourse network that includes the Interpreter and the inhabitants of the House Beautiful, he is still not a skilled enough reader to find his way to the Celestial City on his own. His tour through the Interpreter's house, then, offers an opportunity to practice close reading. In the first rooms, the Interpreter demonstrates how to read the spiritual messages encoded in the symbols of each room.[21] The behavior of the children Passion and Patience, for example, teaches Christian not to covet worldly things but to wait patiently for the rewards of the afterlife. In the first "private Room," the Interpreter explains the symbolic objects in a picture of a man whose "work is to know, and unfold dark things for sinners" (24). As Christian discovers, the man in the picture is Christ, who reveals important information to those who, like Christian, are able to decipher the "dark things" in his message in order to reach salvation (24). Christ has developed the ability to make meaning out of metaphors and pass that meaning along to less skilled readers and listeners, so that effective communication in *Pilgrim's Progress* must be both written and oral in nature. As Brown points out, though the emblems in the Interpreter's House are visual, the Interpreter must verbally tell Christian how to solve them (23).

The Interpreter explains the first scenes to Christian, providing him with a model of reading that he should then be able to mimic on his own. As he moves deeper into the house, he then gradually begins to participate in the explanation of each visual riddle. By the time they approach a palace guarded by a record-keeper and armed men, Christian believes he has practiced enough to decipher the riddle's meaning on his own: "Then Christian smiled and said, I think verily I know the meaning of this" (28). The Interpreter, however, does not yet think Christian is ready to read on his own. "Nay stay," he responds, "till I have shewed thee a little more, and after that, thou shalt go on thy way" (28). Close reading cannot be learned so quickly. To avoid meeting the fate of the men who attempt to push past the guards but are hacked to pieces, Christian must become a confident but not overzealous reader, recognizing his limitations. Christian's lessons in the Interpreter's House are not lessons in reading scripture, Davies finds, but are rather lessons in the kind of experimental interpretation the Bunyan reader must learn to understand *Pilgrim's Progress*. Further, the lessons are meant to be habit changing: Christian and the reader are submersed in the event of interpretation, where the riddles are "events largely indistinguishable from the reality of [Christian's] other encounters beyond the Interpreter's House" (254).[22]

The Interpreter's house, which is made up of a series of locked rooms inaccessible to those without a guide, stands as a fitting metaphor for *Pilgrim's Progress*. Although the secrets of Christian's pilgrimage are revealed by the second part, his wife's journey is a separate wing without a key, because she is introduced to a new series of riddles at the Interpreter's house. She anticipates the meaning of the first room, in which hangs a portrait of a man who covets worldly things and cannot see the man above him, correctly identifying him as "a man of this World" (164). Impressed, the Interpreter accepts her reading and goes on to explain the other symbols in the image (164). When she utters a prayer of deliverance from the man, however, the Interpreter responds: "That Prayer [. . .] has lain by till 'tis almost rusty" (165). In this exchange, the first time he has reprimanded any of his visitors, the Interpreter's tone suddenly changes and, not coincidentally, so do the rooms and riddles he exhibits. As soon as Christiana confidently assumes she understands the meaning of the portrait, the narrative of the second part shifts to criticize the dangers of habitual reading.

At first it seems as though Christiana will pass through the Interpreter's rooms very quickly, already knowledgeable about each riddle's meaning because of her familiarity with the house from stories of her husband's journey. However, the riddles of each room are different from those Christian learned to read. Swaim reads Christiana's access to information about her husband's journey in terms of inheritance, remarking that "the Way of part II is large overdetermined, its events dominated by the meanings inherited from part I" (188). I disagree, however, that Christiana's journey adopts the meanings of her husband's, because as analysis of the episode of the Interpreter's House suggests, the riddles of Christiana's journey, which are not identical to Christian's, pose new challenges to the pilgrims as readers. In a seminar on psychoses, Jacques Lacan describes two scenarios of reading that offer insight into the two pilgrims' encounters in the House of the Interpreter. On the one hand, one may pretend to read without understanding what she is looking at, while on the other she may know a text by heart—as Christiana does—and so never actually read it again. "[W]hat orientates, fundamentally, the point of discourse," Lacan concludes, "is perhaps nothing other than to stay exactly within the limits of what has already been said" (207). Lacan also determines that since the predominance of reading, "there is a permanent discourse that underlies the inscription of what takes place over the course of the subject's history" that "doubles all his acts" (209). Christiana's journey is prompted by that very discourse, since it is her biography of sins that awakens her.

Bunyan scholars often criticize the second part of *Pilgrim's Progress* on the grounds that it merely repeats the first part, that it in fact stays "within the limits of what has already been said" (207). Davies believes Christiana's performance at the Interpreter's House, where she confronts emblems he believes are "deliberately gendered" and "easier to understand," proves that she and her companions are "constantly forgetful" and "intellectually and spiritually inferior" (335). David Mills reads Christiana's journey as repetitious to the point of being mechanical, even going so far as to call the riddles of the Interpreter's

House "exemplary automata" (176–7). Rather than condemn the second part because of its repetition, it may be more productive to consider the idea of mechanization as it parallels the work's concern with reading and interpretation. In the age of mass printing, Bibles, conversion narratives, allegories, and other books can be written, but no one necessarily reads them as they should be read. Literacy, already a complicated social activity because single communities exhibit such varied skill levels and because those communities must learn how to use publicity effectively, becomes even more complex. Another implication of mechanization, for example, is the possibility that documents like scripture or texts like *Pilgrim's Progress* can be counterfeited, misprinted, and misinterpreted. The author's prefatory remarks in the second part specifically address recent instances of plagiarism in which *Pilgrim's Progress* has been printed by others under the same title and even with part of Bunyan's name (136). The practice was not uncommon and authors of the century often mention false copies in their prefaces and apologies, but the narrator's discussion of counterfeiting is particularly important here because it precedes a second book that will repeat Christian's journey, that itself is a copy. One of the unstated tasks of Christiana's journey, indeed, is to provide additional evidence about her husband's, and through his dream of Christiana and her children the narrator retestifies for the first journey. Once the printing press is programmed, in the eighteenth-century sense of the word, by blocks of letters that will stamp each page with the image of words, multiple copies of books can be produced without authors or scribes reading the words as they are written. In this way, reading is no longer simply the ability to decipher "a coded system of visible marks" but the ability to meet the challenges of *automatic* reading, a scenario Lacan does not include in his analysis (Ong 84).

As he recounts his decision to publish *Pilgrim's Progress* in his apology for the first part, Bunyan addresses the distinction between textual misunderstanding and automatic reading. By referring to a dream, a narrative device with biblical and classical precedents that he will use to frame both journeys, Bunyan begins to map out the types of reading that the two parts will consider in more depth:

> Would'st though read Riddles, and their Explanation,
>   Or else be drownded in thy Contemplation?
>   Would'st thou be in a Dream and yet not sleep?
>   Would'st read thy self and read thou know'st not what? (7)

In the first two lines, Bunyan's readers are asked to consider the text closely enough to find the explanations to riddles, to interpret texts—and more importantly, metaphors—as Christian learns to in the Interpreter's house. Much of his apology for the first book anticipates his audience's struggles with metaphor, a poetic device he defends when he asks: "was not Gods Laws, His Gospel-laws in older time held forth By Types, Shadows and Metaphors?" (4). The "explanations" to the riddles are located *in* the text, but Bunyan anticipates that some readers will "drown" themselves in "contemplation" as they attempt to make sense of the figurative language, looking outside the text for applicable meanings. In the last lines he shifts from this interpretive challenge, which fits Lacan's description of the reader who does not understand the text, to the profound disorientation of readers so uncertain of what they are reading that they miss the most important message: that the text is about *them.*[23]

Because her way has already been recorded in town records that are accessible to the community, Christiana's journey does seem mechanized at times. She easily avoids the Mud of Dispond, for example, because she has read the records of Christian's encounter with it. However, though Christiana and her fellow travelers are confident that the secrets of obstacles like Doubting Castle and Vanity Fair will be available to them through circulated documents, their way is not as uneventful as "a delightful ramble through a country from which most of the dangers have been removed" (Sadler 140). In a sense, the narrator's description of the Valley of the Shadow of Death in the first part may serve as a more accurate assessment of Christiana's voyage:

> You must note, that tho the first part of the Valley of the Shadow of Death was dangerous, yet this second part which he was yet to go, was, if possible, far more dangerous: for from the place where he now stood, even to the end of the Valley, the way was all along set so full of Snares, Traps, Gins, and Nets here, and so full of Pits, Pitfalls, and deep holes, and shelvings down there. (53–4)

The narrator's description of the valley relies upon the repetition of synonyms for obstacles that one can fall into or be caught up with. All are dangers of mobility, things to be walked into unaware, and perhaps more importantly, their multiplicity and secret placement mean that they will work numerous times, catching pilgrims on their first walk as well as those on their second. Pilgrims who successfully pass through the first part of the valley may make the fatal mistake of thinking they have mastered the obstacle, that their way will be easy from that point forward. It is at this point, however, that they are most challenged. Just because information is now public does not mean that Christiana knows everything she needs for a safe journey. Likewise, readers of the second part of *Pilgrim's Progress* may assume that interpreting Christiana's journey will be easier because of their practice with the first and because the author takes pains to point out that Christiana is the "key" to her husband's journey. But what the author fails to mention, what he again keeps secret, is that the reader's confidence is the target of his latest project.

Only after Christiana and her companions have been warned about the dangers of habitual and automatic reading can publicized information begin to be effective. Both Davies and Beth Lynch agree that Christiana and her followers represent "model readers" of part one, but it is important to point out that they are not models by nature but by practice and experience (Lynch 157). Though they are now aware that their familiarity with Christian's adventures could cause them to assume too much about their own journey and thus lose their way, they still have several lessons to learn on their journey. Publicity alone still does not lead to successful communication. First, they must learn to adapt the habits of traditional oral discourse to their era's new media. Ong finds that during oral discourse, meaning depends upon situation, what he calls "direct semantic ratification" (47). "The present," he writes, "imposed its own economy on past remembrances" (48). To avoid automatic reading, the pilgrims must find a way to create a similar feeling of presence in written discourse. Ong does not criticize writing or print because it lacks presence; on the contrary, he praises it because the temporal and physical distance between the writer and reader minimizes potential personal conflict: "When all verbal communication must be by direct word of mouth, interpersonal relations are kept high—both attractions and, even more, antagonisms" (45). *Pilgrim's Progress* illustrates this possibility yet shows that written discourse could stand to benefit from the presence of oral tradition. Because writing "separates" words from their "living present," writers must find ways to give their works a sense of immediacy, a memorable quality that readers, who Ong feels lack the strong memories that listeners do, need to recall the story (Ong 82). From the moment they leave the Interpreter's house, then, Christiana's group will witness the unification of written and oral discourse through multimedia scenes that balance distance and presence. Hofmeyr at one point even calls *Pilgrim's Progress* as a whole "multimedia" in nature because it was both read and spoken (27). At once publicly accessible and personally memorable, the last half of the second part depicts a seventeenth-century community that has successfully negotiated traditional and modern communication systems.

Accompanied by Great-Heart, Christiana, her sons, and Mercie follow the path they already know from records of Christian's journey, but at each site they learn new information about what has occurred in the years between the pilgrimages. In Christian's story, for instance, Simple, Sloth, and Presumption lay sleeping after taking a shortcut; when Christiana finds them, however, their bodies are on public display on the scaffold, where they have been hung for crimes they committed between the years of the two journeys.[24] Christiana asks Great-Heart why a written warning does not stand in place of the corpses, like the warning Christian and Hopeful erect outside the property lines of Doubting Castle. He answers that there is a sign "you well may perceive if you will go a little to the Wall" (177). In her study, Lynch believes that the mutilated and tortured corpses "heighten an impression of alternative planes of experience and existence" and emphasize the connection between doubt and violence only hinted at in the first part (162). Another way to read this scene is that it demonstrates how violent images can act as safeguards against habitual reading, as gruesome reminders to pay closer attention to the lessons of scripture. A public sign is not enough to deter pilgrims who pass, but an additional marker—three dead bodies—provides visual motivation. In other words, the bodies make the lesson more memorable. In a similar rhetorical move, Great-Heart exhibits the head of the Giant Despair on a pole "right over against the Pillar that Christian erected for a Caution to Pilgrims that came after, to take heed of entering into his Grounds" (236).[25] The decapitated head indicates that the giant's property has been completely destroyed: secret traps like Doubting Castle cannot exist in a network in which pilgrims communicate so easily and quickly with one another.[26] Systems that depend completely upon secrecy to work "fit in with the existing forms of communication without difficulty as long as the decisive element—publicness—[is] lacking" (Habermas 16). Located on an increasingly busy road, his rural property is overrun with traffic to the Celestial City, and the dangers of trespassing are advertised to all who pass. The property of Doubting Castle has become an interstate.

The Slow of Despond, The Interpreter's House, and House Beautiful all occupy neighborhoods located within walking distance of the Celestial City, but while citizens of the distant City of Destruction can communicate with and eventually join residents of the Celestial City, citizens of those areas nearest heaven are barred from crossing city lines. Distant societies communicate with one another easily and with great speed, but geographical neighbors keep within strict boundaries. Christian's journey is compartmentalized by sites of visitation, and each location maintains an autonomous landscape with individually controlled channels of communication.[27] By the middle of Christiana's journey, however, neighborhoods communicate more easily with one another. At the end of her visit with Humble-mind, Charity, Prudence, and Piety, for example, Christiana sends a post from the House Beautiful to the House of the Interpreter, asking permission for Great-Heart to accompany her party all the way to the Celestial City. The Interpreter's response is almost immediate. When "he had seen the contents of the Petitions," he instantly "said to the Messenger, Go tell them that I will send him" (192). His quick understanding and instant response are a contrast to the earlier episode in which Christiana is visited by her neighbors. Not only must they visit her in person, but they must also struggle to understand her. Christiana's journey, then, traces the progression of a communication system. In the beginning, it cannot sustain the "fatal diversity of human language," as Anderson puts it, but by the end of the journey both dispersed and localized residents can communicate easily with one another.

Christiana takes one important detour that her husband did not experience on his journey. Tired from their walk, Christian, Mercie and the children stop for the night at the house of Gaius, an inn-keeper. As soon as they become acquainted and Gaius learns that Christiana is Christian's wife, he begins describing the history of the family's lineage, hoping at the conclusion that the sons "will bear up their Fathers Name, and tread in their Fathers steps, and come to their Fathers end" (216). "Christian's Family is like still to spread abroad upon the face of the Ground, and yet to be numerous upon the Face of the Earth," Gaius remarks, and Honesty responds, "'Tis pity this Family should fall and be extinct" (217). Lamenting the ultimate breakdown of the family line, the group decides that Mercie will marry Christiana's son and stay behind, on the road to the Celestial City, to raise a family. The area, once habitable only by characters like the Interpreter and the Giant Despair, is now suburbia, a residential neighborhood just outside the city limits. As Eisenstein notes, "even while communal solidarity was diminished, vicarious participation in more distant events was also enhanced; and even while local ties were loosened, links to larger collective units were being forged" (132). By staying behind, Mercie helps to build a new community along a highly-trafficked route, and she also serves as a direct connection to the city. Citizens can now relocate and live far from their family and friends because modern communication technologies like the postal system allow them to keep in touch with their loved ones.

As she nears the end of her journey, Christiana is accompanied by other pilgrims in the area whose journeys all seem to converge with hers. During the series of meetings that follow, the group grows to include Christiana, her four sons, Great-Heart, Honest, Feeble-mind, Ready-to-hault, Dispondencie, and Much-Afraid. Christiana's presence, in fact, is a highly publicized event. Citizens call out in the streets that "More Pilgrims are come to Town" and speak excitedly to one another (254). The community anticipates the group's arrival, conversing about their predicted appearance, and it also records the pilgrims' names in writing. The scene is a sharp contrast to Christian and Hopeful's final moments. When they reach the Celestial City, they read the sign written above the gate and offer their certificates, which are then "carried into the King, who when he had read them," admits them into the city (132). Immediately behind them Ignorance arrives, and though he passes all the tests on the pilgrimage and even crosses the river with less difficulty than Christian, he is turned away from the Celestial City because he neither carries a certificate from the King nor reads the sign on the gate. The narrator stops to point out that Ignorance merely "looked up at the writing that was above," with the implication that he does not take time to read it (133). The ending to the first part, then, emphasizes the ultimate division between the literate and illiterate. Texts are matters of survival. But in the ending to the second part, the oral, once symptomatic of illiteracy, and the written, once the medium of alienation, work cooperatively, and the publicized event unites rather than divides the community.

The narrator does not emphasize whether or not Christiana's journey will be recorded and passed on to successors as he does with her husband's pilgrimage. Instead, in the wife's journey he places more emphasis on the pilgrimage as media event. The delivery of the post, for example, becomes a public event: "there was a Noyse in the Town, that there was a Post come from the Celestial City, with Matter of great Importance, to one Christiana" (255). The "true messenger" greets Christiana and, though there is no reason why he cannot deliver the message verbally, hands her a letter stating that she will soon be called to the city. To prove that the text is authentic, he then pricks her with an arrow "sharpened by love" (255). Ten days later, Christiana receives the final letter beckoning her to cross the river into the Celestial City, and unlike her husband's road, which he and Hopeful traveled alone, Christiana's road to the river is "full of People to see her take her Journey" (257). Nothing is anticipated in the town as much as the return of the postal carrier. In the last moments of the second part, a succession of letters is delivered to each of the pilgrims, so that the arrival of the post signals another death, the delivery of deliverance.

The second part's foregrounding of distance communication through post and print clarify Bunyan's use of framing devices, which critics have up until now dismissed as the narrative mistakes of a novice author. In the beginning of the second part, the narrator claims to take a trip to the town he dreamed of in the first part, but when he has only a mile remaining he falls asleep in the woods. Dreaming, he meets Sagacity, and the two walk the rest of the way to the town together as Sagacity recounts Christiana's journey (143). A frame within a frame, then, Christiana's journey is told by a narrator who travels to the site of the story only to fall asleep, experience a dream vision, and then learn of the story through conversation. In this way, Bunyan makes two seemingly incompatible types of discourse work together to tell a story. Communication from a distance, here actually the distance of one mile, is paired with conversation, communication on the most intimate local level.

Unlike the narrative of the first part of *Pilgrim's Progress,* of which the anonymous narrator is an eye witness and records from within a dream vision, the narrative of the second part is framed as a conversation *within* a dream vision. In both parts the narrator is a silent listener, remembering everything he hears so that he can write it all down later, but in the second he dreams of conversation; all information about Christiana's journey is filtered through Sagacity. After dreaming of Christian's journey, the narrator records in writing what he sees and hears in his dream, but after Christiana's journey he must transcribe what he cannot see, the words relayed to him during a private exchange with an informed citizen. And though the second part is staged entirely as a conversation, the narrator never participates in the exchange. The shift between recording by sight and transcription by sound parallels the work's larger move from the private reading of public documents, like the Bible, to the public reading of private documents, like letters and autobiographies. Between the dream and the conversation, the trip to the city and the pause one mile from its entrance, the narrative frame of the second part imitates the work's broader concern with the balance of emerging information systems like post and print, which allow distance communication through traveling documents and exchange with strangers, and systems on which human communication has always relied and through which families pass down their histories for future generations.

The narrator imagines a global network of readers connected by the common experience of reading *Pilgrim's Progress.* As first evidenced by Christian's abandonment of his family, communities are not necessarily connected by the act of reading or, if all members are literate, with the experience of reading a common text, like the Bible. Even under one roof residents are not necessarily part of the same discourse network. In a moment of self-advertisement, the author describes his global reading audience, an audience with members from around the world who are united by his text: "My Pilgrims Book has travel'd Sea and Land," he writes, and as far as he knows it has never disappointed readers in locales as diverse as Flanders, the Highlands, New England, and Holland (138). While the apology to the first part describes the final decision to print his manuscript, the second describes the

immense readership of the publication, revealing that within a few short
years the printed work has reached across oceans and to countless readers.[28]

In both stories of *Pilgrim's Progress,* Bunyan identifies the protagonist's
journey with the book itself, so that the pilgrims' trial and pursuit of the
Celestial City is aligned with the book's writing, publication, and reception
by its readership. But while in the first apology Bunyan admits that readers
must expend considerable effort to seek out, find, and understand the book
and its message, the second apology presents the book as a portable, widely
accessible commodity:

> GO, now my little Book, to every place,
> > Where my first Pilgrim has but shewn his Face,
> > Call at their door: If any say, who's there?
> > Then answer thou, Christiana is here. (135)

Bunyan animates his text as he did in the apology to the first part, but this
time he issues a command to his book to deliver itself directly to the
doorsteps of readers. Such a summons is not uncommon in literature before
Pilgrim's Progress, but the contrast between the first and second apologies
reveals that Bunyan gains a better understanding of how print technology
works—that he adjusts and adapts to it, as McLuhan puts it. Like the King
of the Celestial City, Bunyan authenticates his message and recognizes the
benefits of sending it out to readers who choose to read it. Virtual communities joined by books and mail routes are substituted for communities
dependent only upon local correspondence.

Pilgrim's Progress proves that even as early as 1678, the perceptual consequences of mechanical reproduction through print were already apparent.
From the first dream in which Christiana is visited by the divine messenger,
Secret, to her final invitation to the Celestial City by post, the second part is
written for readers who are curious to understand the secrets of the first part.
In the end, Christiana's journey represents a community that depends upon a
balance of the oral and the written, the public and the secret, print and the
postal system, to survive. Members communicate avidly with one another via
documents transported great distances, and by reading the documents members are privy to secrets totally inaccessible to those outside the network. The
break between the first and second parts, then, marks the difference between
early and later seventeenth-century attitudes toward information systems.

Chapter Two

Information as Ambush:
Miscommunication and the Post in
Behn's *The History of the Nun*

In the last scene of Aphra Behn's *The History of the Nun: or, The Fair Vow-Breaker,* the young Isabella de Valerie stands on a scaffold before "the whole world," prepared for her decapitation. In the final moments before the death sentence she "joyfully received" is carried out, Isabella confronts a public that, up until this point, has represented a distant, faceless communication network (257). Before she kneels down for the executioner, Isabella removes her veil so that the large group of townspeople who have gathered to witness her death can see her face for the first time. The vow-breaker's decisions, first to speak to the spectators from behind a veil and, second, to unveil for the moment of decapitation, highlight the novel's concern with the concealment and disclosure of information and the incompatibility of the two modes of discourse that drive the action of the history—the discourse of the vow and the developing discourse of public news in Isabella's late seventeenth-century information society.[1]

What Eisenstein observed more than twenty years ago is still generally true: "We hear much about the effects of the commercial revolution but nothing about those of the communications revolution" (30). Behn's *History,* which has received relatively little attention in comparison to works like *Oroonoko* and *The Rover,* is usually discussed either within the context of the era's political climate or the author's feminist project.[2] Politically, Janet Todd postulates that "the Church here stands in for the King, whose subjects would follow Isabella at their peril," and that the "overwhelming message that emerges from the *History* is Behn's conviction that inclinations change"

(393). Similarly, Rosalind Ballaster reads the *History* as a commentary on the exclusion crisis. Jacqueline Pearson and Jane Spencer approach the *History* from feminist perspectives. Pearson concludes that Behn "seeks to explain the social origins of what is conventionally read as female wickedness and to allow a woman to satisfy her own desires without necessarily being seen as evil" (250). Both Pearson and Spencer speculate that Isabella serves as metaphor for the woman writer, who is cornered by social rules of behavior incompatible with the realities of the age.[3] Spencer sees the nun figure in Behn's fiction as a version of Behn herself, and she points to moments during which Behn seems to interrupt the exposition or narrative to state her association with the female protagonist, such as in the *History* when the narrator claims that she is personally unable to make the religious promise that Isabella agrees to (170). In the end, Spencer accepts Behn's *History* as a lesson for those who break religious vows (128).[4]

Todd, Ballaster, Pearson, and Spencer's readings, although helpful, do not account for the novel's obvious concern with communication and the unstable transmission of messages, oral and written, between its characters. Eisenstein's discoveries, as well as those of other scholars now assessing the history of communications technologies, invite readers to consider the *History* as it challenges assumptions about the effectiveness of the era's information systems. Isabella's panicked decision to murder both of her husbands results not simply from the restrictive female sphere, as Todd and Pearson argue, but also from Isabella's fear that news of her double marriage will be disclosed to the public and used to control her.

Throughout the novel, Isabella's private life is subject to the scrutiny of a public that receives frequent information about her through anonymous records and reports. Letters, however, serve perhaps the most significant narrative function in the novel, driving the plot, complicating Isabella's already difficult life, and sealing her fate in the final dramatic scenes. Significantly, the movement of letters parallels the movement of wealth in the *History*, so that mail routes reflect inheritance lines through which characters are either connected to or completely cut off from their property birthrights. More broadly, the transference of letters almost always takes place in terms of economic exchange. The opening dedication, for example, is a letter sent to secure the patronage of Hortense Mancini, the Duchess of Mazarine and one of Charles II's many mistresses. The last letter of the novel, sent via a prisoner of war who accompanies Isabella's first husband on his journey home, contains only a name and address, linking the addressee with his property and, as a result, delivering the fatal news that finally condemns Isabella to the scaffold.

The perpetual transmission of mail in the novel prompts readers to wonder how message-delivery systems of the late seventeenth century were structured. By looking first at contemporary improvements in the British postal service and the connection between the Post Office and espionage as representative of general anxiety about potentially subversive, private news, readers can better understand the role of the post in the novel, particularly as it highlights legal dilemmas of inheritance and political promise-making. Throughout Behn's novel, posts disappear in mid-delivery, communicate false or misleading information, and in the end corner Isabella in a sudden ambush against which she cannot defend herself except by actively participating in the subversive exchange as secret agent.

Isabella's decision to become a nun is reported almost immediately to the town she leaves behind (216). An admirer, Villenoys, writes to her daily, and news of her marriage to her first husband, Henault, "was spread over all the town and country" (239). Such a system, which allowed daily communication not only between large towns but also between towns and rural residences, was not available to the public much before the decades of Behn's writing. Pre-seventeenth-century postal services, like the earliest Roman message delivery methods, were not organized systems but conveniences for citizens with the luxury of a personal courier, and they usually died with the prominent figures who started them. Such services were never for public use and, in most countries, maintained solely for the benefit of government figures or royal families (Robinson 67). It was not until the seventeenth century that a public postal service developed and, upon the return of Charles II, the first law to establish the Post Office as an official government body was passed. James How summarizes the consequences simply: "What the Post Office did was bring about a whole new level of connectivity" (7).[5]

During and after the Revolution of 1688 and as Behn wrote the *History*, deliveries by postal carriers increased dramatically as more citizens used the mail service to communicate. As How finds, however, not everyone was enthusiastic about government control of the mail and the public nature of its transmission: "for those aristocrats and gentry used to the cocooning feeling provided by the private carriage of letters by trusted and known carriers, the Post Office generated a new and perhaps uncomfortable feeling" (4). What seemed intrusive to some citizens was liberating for others, How finds. How sees the Post Office as particularly empowering for women writers, for example, because it created a "forum in which women [could] participate in the world of politics and take risks" (17). Sending letters by private carrier, in contrast, generally meant that a woman's mail was ultimately controlled by her father or husband, as How finds was the case with avid letter-writer

Dorothy Osborne. In Behn's *History*, it is worth noting that while readers cannot know whether letters to Isabella definitely come by the Post Office, there is no mention of a private carrier. Some letters, however, are delivered personally by the men who write them, so that Isabella's mail is in one sense even more controlled than it would have been if her husband employed a private courier.

Because many wealthy citizens refused to use the system and opted instead to keep their own carriers on staff, late seventeenth-century government officials became very concerned about "secret conveyance" and illegal transmission by private couriers operating independently of the developing government service (67). The business of secret conveyance figures into both the life of Behn and the *History*. Todd discovers that Behn was personally involved in the dangerous business of espionage, which relies upon the transmission and interception of secret messages in order to further a political or social agenda (*Secret* 31). As a courier during and after the Revolution, Behn worked outside of the law, transporting, relaying, and intercepting information for her royalist employers.

Even in its early years, the Post Office was financially profitable, but "the receipts were used for almost every purpose except the improvement of the service" (Robinson 53). For example, the Duchess of Cleveland, another mistress of Charles II, received a large pension from the postal fund, and the future Queen Anne received £5000 annually as part of her dowry (53). In the case of the Duchess of Cleveland, profits from the service were passed on to her illegitimate son, the Duke of Grafton, and then to his children, until the pension was finally revoked in 1856 (78). An only child of a widower, Isabella stands to inherit a considerable sum, and this inheritance becomes an incentive for the nuns to keep her in the convent. Inheritance occupies an important although understated presence in the *History*, and interruptions in the patriarchal line of inheritance occur concurrently with interruptions in distance communication.[6]

Read within the developing legal and political framework of the British postal system, the *History* offers commentary on the era's fastest growing information technology—the postal system—which promises to open communication between private citizens yet is rooted in secrecy and political deception. As Ballaster reads it, the *History* refers to the Popish Plot and its effect on the discourse of promise-making. The Popish Plot, of course, was revealed only because a citizen's message about it was intercepted by an agent working to detect conspiracies against the crown. Isabella's violation of the vow, religious or marital, is part of a larger framework of "double dealing" in the novel that is much like the work of the hired spy. Messengers in the *History* work covertly, manipulating information for their own purposes, usually financial. During the course of the novel, Isabella undergoes a transformation: when she is young she is domestic property passed on with the family inheritance, but when the inheritance is lost and she is no longer financially valuable she becomes a post in the system, an intercepted letter that never finds its way to its final destination.

Readers are made aware, through the narrator's frequent remarks about public reaction to Isabella's activities, that they are part of an audience. Her story evolves as a local news event and is punctuated by publicly-circulated records and reports. Before the story begins, for example, the narrator explains in her dedication to Hortense Mancini that it "is true, as it is on the records of the town where it was transacted" (211). The narrator repeatedly describes the effect of Isabella's decisions on the public in hyperbole: when she goes abroad her "virtues were the discourse of all the world," news of her return to the convent is "spread all over the town" to the "heart-breaking of a thousand lovers," and her rejection of Villenoys "was the whole discourse of the town" (216–217). Henault and Isabella's bad luck after their forbidden marriage becomes a town proverb, for "all over the country if any ill luck had arrived to anybody, they would say, 'They had Monsieur Beroon's luck'" (240). Isabella is under constant surveillance by a public that is never identified except as the "whole world," and the narrator's sensitivity to public reaction intensifies the narrative focus.

Isabella is surrounded by characters who operate covertly and strategically withhold or plant information to dictate her decisions. As a relay between father and daughter, Isabella's aunt, the Lady Abbess of the convent, controls and manipulates information in order to appropriate the considerable inheritance that accompanies Isabella if she remains. The aunt thinks of her niece purely in terms of a transaction: in exchange for taking care of her after her mother's death and during her father's mourning, the aunt puts the convent in a position to gain additional wealth. Her strategy is to exaggerate the wonders of town life to such an extent that the reality will be a disappointment. She "would very often discourse to [Isabella] of the pleasures of the world," the narrator recounts, "telling her how much happier she would think herself to be the wife of some gallant cavalier" and "to live in splendor, to eat high, and wear magnificent clothes, to be bowed to as she passed, and have a thousand adorers" (215). When she does visit town, Isabella is courted by many, but "nothing created wonder in her, though never so strange and novel" and she "surveyed all things with an indifference" (216). The actual experience of the world pales next to the town her aunt has described.

Kittler concludes that "[i]nformation technology is always already strategy or war" (*Discourse* 371). The aunt may not use obvious information technologies like print or post, but she does persuade Isabella to remain in the convent by mimicking the discourse of her information society, exaggerating the wonders of town life to such an extent that the reality can never live up to the extravagant descriptions Isabella has been given. By misreporting what life outside the convent has to offer, the aunt perjures herself as she speaks, manipulating Isabella to remain in the convent while all the while appearing to persuade her to leave it for the wonders of town life. Her strategy is not to withhold information about the town, but rather to overload Isabella with it.

Inside of the convent is the aunt's calculated account of life in town, but outside is town discourse, an endless circulation of messages that are transformed as they are transmitted between senders and receivers. Though the only important message in the convent should be the divine one, the nuns, nearly cut off from the circulation of public information, beg visitors to bring them news of "all that was novel in the town" (235). Henault, for example, one of the nuns' favorite messengers, "told 'em all he could either remember, or invent, to please 'em" (235). As his inventive relay reveals, senders who put messages or "news" into circulation take liberty with content and may not hesitate to fictionalize their descriptions. Claire Walker would not be surprised by the nuns' insatiable interest in town news and their ability to receive reports despite their isolation. In her helpful study of the seventeenth-century convent, Walker finds that Isabella and the other nuns in the convent are in a historically difficult position. On one hand, they depend upon "open channels of communication," particularly postal ones, to help them negotiate finances and reach women they wish to recruit (161). On the other hand, due to stricter rules under the Catholic Church after 1563 with the Council Trent, nuns were supposed to completely isolate themselves from society after taking their vows (161). Mail was strictly limited and censored, even to and from family. Walker finds, however, that many nuns continued to correspond by mail and frequently wrote letters despite more extreme limitations; in fact, "religious women exchanged news, discussed the settlement of kin, negotiated dowries, pursued creditors, and sought patronage" by letter (160). While Isabella is not an avid letter writer, a fact that conflicts with Walker's findings, Isabella's aunt fits Walker's portrait perfectly.[7]

The narrator's description of the convent and the town it communicates with reveals that the public discourse of Iper works very quickly, a fast-forward genealogy in which messages prompt the creation of infinitely more messages. Iper is "the world," a microcosm of universal exchange in which messages move between all residents. Isabella's return to the convent is passed on as bad news. The narrator's description focuses on the townspeople's *reactions* to her disappearance, and their reactions are always to send more messages, whether "songs of complaint" or the works of wits (216). As she withdraws to the convent, "the whole world that passed through Iper, of strangers, came directed and recommended to the lovely Isabella" (219). Removed from public view, the town becomes even more obsessed with her, so that the *History* suggests that information that is withheld from the public is most interesting, not the excessive and sensationalized news that permeates the town discourse. Historically, then, restrictions imposed by the Catholic Church propagate the very behavior they are designed to deter.

The vow, in contrast to the multiplicity of gossip and the news report, is a single message that must be delivered in earnest, yet like town discourse vows are public promises. Fiction and invention, as Henault demonstrates when he talks with the nuns, is not appropriate within the discourse of the vow. And unlike public messages that circulate widely and change as they move through audiences, the vow should be taken only once and its meaning preserved over time without change (8). Hannah Arendt explains that "[a]ll political business is, and always has been, transacted within an elaborate framework of ties and bonds for the future—such as laws and constitutions, treaties and alliances—all of which derive in the last instance from the faculty to promise and to keep promises in the face of the essential uncertainties of the future" (164). In its juxtaposition of the vow and the public discourse of gossip, news, and letters, the *History* challenges assumptions that personal and institutional structures can remain stable when the two guiding discourses of a community are so at odds with one another. An information society like Isabella's, becoming increasingly obsessed with mass accessibility and the speedier transmission of novel printed and oral information, is a discourse network seemingly incompatible with discourses of tradition and authority like the vow. As Behn's narrator remarks, the "resolution we promise and believe we shall maintain is not in our power" (4).

Isabella is given no option but to choose between vows, yet the information system of "the world" around her is rooted in multiplicity and the infinite reproduction of messages (215).[8] Though vows should only be made once, they are uttered countless times throughout the *History*, so that each crisis in the plot is prompted by a vow or promise that contradicts all those made before it. The vow as communication act, then, becomes infected by the multiplicity inherent in late-seventeenth-century information systems of news and post, in the process destroying its own meaning, credibility, and future. Not coincidentally, the main conflict of the novel is that Isabella ends up with two husbands—or, in political terms, with two allegiances—instead of one. When taken too often, vows mean nothing. In her opening, the narrator explains that "if it were searched into, we should find these frequent perjuries that pass in the world for so many gallantries only, to be the occasion of so many unhappy marriages and the cause of all those misfortunes which are so frequent to the nuptialed pair" (211). In the passages that follow, the narrator speaks often of "numbers" and "a thousand vows" (211). It is not the broken vow that is most disheartening for the narrator but the loss of meaning that comes from taking vows too frequently.

Throughout the *History*, news is described in "fatal" terms and disease metaphors, emphasizing the covert and dangerous nature of the system in which the messages travel. Like a virus, news spreads across the town, moving in invisible channels through the town and surfacing periodically. Most dangerous are messages that report Isabella's disappearances from public scrutiny. [9] Villenoys, for example, tries to keep updated on "the fatal ceremony of Isabella's being made a nun," preparing himself for delivery of news that is described as a violent blow to his body's immune system: "They assured her, Villenoys was dying, and dying adoring her; that nothing could save his life but her kind eyes turned upon the fainting lover" (218). The nuns, who act as mediators between the two lovers, decide what information to pass on and how to modify it to diminish Villenoys's suffering. News of Isabella's ceremony "was carefully concealed," the narrator writes, "so that in a little time he recovered his lost health, at least so well as to support the fatal news, and upon the first hearing it, he made ready his equipage and departed immediately for Candia" (217, 219). In this way, the manipulation of discourse allows his immune system to recover enough so that he can withstand news of Isabella's vow when he finally hears of it. Concealment is therefore dangerous, triggering a sequence of life-threatening events, yet it is also a counterstrategy, offering an antidote for poisonous messages.

Villenoys's departure for Candia after falling ill from the near "fatal news" highlights Behn's sophisticated commentary on the role of information during an era fraught with political and social disorder (219). Here, the narrative shifts quickly from *news* to the *news event,* and war signals the ultimate failure of communication that readers also see acted out on a domestic and local stage. The battlefield is the violent site at which human lives are exchanged for political gain of wealth or property. In 1667, for example, Venice asked for European help with its war against invading Turkish troops (*Secret* 120). England agreed to assist but only with the stipulation that its aid would be covert, since Parliament believed that knowledge of English assistance would prompt Turkey to destroy important merchant posts in the East (120). As the *History* implies, France also may have agreed to assist

Venice. Such a move would have threatened French-English relations. Todd finds that "the [English] government suspected the French of reneging on their promise to disarm in the recent peace by pretending to send a force of soldiers to the help of Venice" (120). Behn may have been sent on a spy mission to Venice to verify or discredit reports of French military participation (120). The Turkish-Venetian war in the background of the *History's* plot reiterates a larger political connection between message relay and strategy evident in the aunt's smaller-scale manipulation of information for financial gain. As Todd's overview reveals, the presence of war also adds to the narrator's commentary on the broken promise; English anxiety over whether or not France would break its promise to them parallels the novel's concern for broken domestic vows.

In Behn's *History*, the message will misreport death and, as a result, will become part of an unfolding news event that will be reported to others. Similarly, Kittler observes that personal stories and histories are inevitably connected because "[a]ll the orders and judgements, announcements and prescriptions (military and legal, religious and medical) that produced mountains of corpses were communicated [in] the very same channel that monopolized the descriptions of those mountains of corpses" (*Gramophone* 4). Lèvy reaches a similar conclusion in his work on virtual reality, pointing out that information technologies do not report "the event itself but a message about the event," so that "while the event itself is actual, the production and distribution of messages about it constitute a virtualization of the event" (74). Especially during the early years of the postal system when only six rural branches extended out from the central London office, the sheer number of messages could overwhelm the channels in which they traveled. Messages were frequently lost, intercepted, and delivered to the wrong addressees. Message delivery became an adventure in its own right. The *History's* plot, for example, pivots not on a war, a scandal, or some other newsworthy narrative moment but on the delivery of two letters.

Much like a postal communication that becomes news event, the vow is a "speech act that [is], and only can be, accomplished in the statement" (Deleuze and Guattari 79). However, Deleuze and Guattari argue that the news report differs from a speech act like the vow because news is usually "a relation of redundancy" (79). "Newspapers, news," Deleuze and Guattari state, "proceed by redundancy, in that they tell us what we 'must' think, retain, expect, etc. Language is neither informational nor communicational" (79). Yet news is interesting only if it is new; old news is no news at all. Deleuze and Guattari do not make the point, but in their analysis it is the receiver's reaction to the news that is redundant, not the message. For a reader to think or retain what the news relays, she must receive some type of new information that prompts her to think differently than she did before reading the message. Redundancy occurs only if new information is included. Perhaps the most important function of the vow, in contrast, is that its message is redundant. The vow must always remain the same, in order to secure the same behavior continuously. In this way, it prepares vow-takers for new situations and information that could tempt them to betray their promises. Vows depend upon redundancy to operate, because without the temptation of new and unexpected situations there would be no need to take them. At the same time, they are continually threatened by the new. In the *History*, the vow is tested repeatedly by surprise, and its inability to help the vow-taker "withstand the greatest assaults of fate," the multiple collisions of public discourse and private promise, mark its failure (13).

Isabella's messenger and confidante in the convent, Katteriena, tests the vow's ability to anticipate surprise encounters with new information. Katteriena serves two purposes in the narrative: she demonstrates for Isabella the effectiveness of the surprise encounter as strategic informational ambush, and she teaches her the art of not being read, or dissemblage. During a conversation about "pictures and likenesses," for example, Katteriena tosses a picture of her brother, Henault, at the unsuspecting Isabella (221). Upon seeing it, Isabella swoons in proper romantic fashion and then launches into a one-sentence defense of her reaction:

> My dearest sister, I do confess, I was surprised at the sight of Monsieur Henault, and much more than ever you have observed me to be at the sight of his person, because there is scarce a day wherein I do not see that, and know beforehand I shall see him; I am prepared for the encounter and have lessened my concern, or rather confusion, by that time I come to the grate, so much mistress I am of my passions when they give me warning of their approach, and sure I can withstand the greatest assaults of fate, if I can but foresee it; but if it surprise me, I find I am as feeble a woman as the most unresolved; you did not tell me you had this picture, nor say you would show me such a picture; but when I least expect to see that face, you show it me, even in my chamber. (221)[10]

Isabella describes the surprise appearance of Henault's picture as an "assault" and accuses Katteriena of withholding information from her, interpreting Katteriena's behavior as covert and threatening. Already in the narrative, new information threatens the vow as stable discourse, and it does so through the language of concealment and disclosure.[11] Isabella realizes that to keep her vow she must overcome the passion she feels when caught off guard. "Inform me, oh! Inform me," she exclaims, "of the nature of that cruel disease, and how thou found'st a cure?" (222). Katteriena's tactic is not to overcome the passion but merely to pretend as though she has, and Isabella must learn how to "dissemble," to control how others read her as Katteriena has already mastered the art (224).[12]

Katteriena never "informs" Isabella of the cure for the disease of love. Thus Isabella must train herself, as a reader, to ward off potentially dangerous messages because the medium of transmission cannot filter out fatal from nonfatal information. In order to prepare herself for moments like her encounter with Henault's portrait, for example, Isabella learns how to "dissemble" (224). "[N]ow contented and joyful beyond imagination to find herself beloved," Isabella decides she should "dissemble her own passion and make him the first aggressor; the first that loved, or at least, that should seem to do so" (227). Isabella does not die from the cruel disease of information, but instead she recovers by learning how to control how and by whom she is read:

> "And are you sure," (said Dame Katteriena) "that this wanton deity is repelled by the noble force of your resolution? Is he never to return?" "No," (replied Isabella) "never to my heart." "Yes," (said Katteriena) "if you should see the lovely murderer of your repose, your wound would bleed anew." (228)

Katteriena, who becomes a messenger between the two, asks if Henault has promised not to return to visit Isabella, but Isabella responds by stating that she is no longer in love with him.[13] Katteriena then tests Isabella's dissemblage when she reveals that Henault is "raving in love" with her, but Isabella passes with convincing disinterest: "the masterpiece of this young maid's art was shown in this minute, for she commanded herself so well that her very looks dissembled and showed no concern at a relation that made her soul dance with joy" (228). She learns how to conceal the love affair because the medium of communication available does not allow private correspondence between the lovers. The *History*, then, raises questions about what media are appropriate for the transmission of private information, particularly private information with substantial public appeal.

In the eyes of the convent and Henault's affluent family, the couple "transgresses the law" when they marry, and as Katteriena warns they become town discourse (239). Under the watchful public eye, they move far from town, change their name to Beroon, and attempt to reconcile with their families (239). The messages they send are never answered. Isabella, for example, "writ her aunt the most moving letters in the world" and "so did Henault to his father; but she was a long time before she could gain so much as an answer from her aunt, and Henault was so unhappy as never to gain one from his father" (239). The father, in fact, "no sooner heard the news that was spread over all the town and country that young Henault was fled with the so famed Isabella" than he strips Henault of his inheritance and gives the family estate to the youngest son (27). Again, familial inheritance is linked to a break in communication, and the couple that is most *in* the news is cut off from it. Henault does receive word of his lost inheritance, but the narrator does not explain how that message reaches him.[14] All she states is that the "news, you may believe, was not very pleasing to the young man" (239). Communication opens at the same time that inheritance is re-established. For example, when Henault decides, against Isabella's wishes, that the only way to regain his father's love and birthright is to join either the Venetian mission against the Turks or the French army, he is rewarded two thousand crowns (242). When he first explains his idea, Isabella suffers a miscarriage (241). Her miscarriage is an interruption, and her failure to deliver stands in stark contrast to the fertile public discourse in which one report "begat" another (216). An adaptation of the *History* by Southerne, *The Fatal Marriage, or, The Innocent Adultery* (1694), deletes Isabella's miscarriage and replaces it with the healthy birth of a son (Pearson 236). The succession of messages is linked with inheritance as a means of familial transmission from which Isabella is cut off first with her mother's death and then with the death of her unborn child.

The central conflict in the novel between the transmission of messages and inheritance is reflected by the town in which Isabella's conflicts occur. As readers are informed early in the narrative, Iper is also property passed from one country to another during the war in which Henault participates to win back his inheritance. "[A] town not long since in the dominions of the King of Spain," the narrator explains, Iper is "now in the possession of the King of France" (213). Apparently because of a contract between the two nations, Iper changes hands as fulfillment of a political promise. Henault joins the army of the former owner, France, suggesting Iper's resentment of being disinherited from its native country and claimed by Spain. Transferred from one nation to another, Iper, like Isabella, is a disinherited orphan with a questionable future, a piece of property with an ambiguous allegiance. And as Tim Stretton reminds readers, many women of the seventeenth century were like prisoners of war as soon as they married: they lacked legal identities, gave up control of their property, and lost any rights to profit, interest, or financial independence (42).

The narrator cuts short her description of the outside material world, interrupting the narration to state: "it is not my business to relate the history of the war" (242). Drawing a line between what she will and will not report, the narrator keeps to local and private news only and leaves the global news of war to others. Lennard Davis's work on truth claims in the developing novel form suggests that the narrator may bow out of war commentary here because fact occupies an awkward position within a fiction that asserts historical truth. "At stake was the capability of narrative to carry the burden of factuality and reliability," Davis writes (37). Also, the narrator makes a point to inform the reader that she is about to withhold information just as she begins describing the most pivotal scene in the novel. In the moments that follow she quickly outlines the context of Henault's alleged death in battle, but she implies that since she is "wholly unacquainted with the terms of battles," her description may not be as accurate as history (242). The scene that follows is the only one in which the narration is filtered through a character other than Isabella. From Villenoys's perspective, the narrator explains that:

> [T]hey were ambushed, in the pursuit of the party of the enemies, and being surrounded, Villenoys had the unhappiness to see his gallant friend fall, fighting and dealing of wounds all around him, even as he descended to the earth, for he fell from his horse at the same moment that he killed a Turk; and Villenoys could neither assist him, nor had he the satisfaction to be able to rescue his dead body from under the horses, but with much ado escaping with his own life got away in spite of all that followed him. (243)

Henault falls during a surprise attack that parallels the scene in which Katteriena throws her brother's portrait at Isabella, and Villenoys and the others are unable to see his body to confirm his death because he is concealed by the horses that have fallen on top of him. Villenoys sees him fall, but he does not see him die. He leaves the battle almost immediately and returns to town, certain that Henault has died but unwilling to "hazard [to] the living the unnecessary services to the dead" (243). He immediately writes to Isabella informing her that Henault has died in battle.[15] Isabella also receives a letter from General Beaufort, who writes of Henault's honor and exclaims that his memory will be eternalized "with the last gasp of his life"—a gasp both the General and Villenoys fail to mention they never witnessed (243). The General mentions that Henault "fell fighting for the Holy Cross," a description that sets Henault up as a martyr despite the fact that he joined the war effort only to appease his father and win back his inheritance (243).

Among the few critics who have analyzed the *History*, none discuss Villenoys's role in the miscommunication of Henault's death or suspect him of intentionally misreporting Henault's status in order to inherit the woman he once pursued. Whatever his motives, Villenoys fails to witness the moment of Henault's death yet testifies to its occurrence. Like the narrator, who immediately pulls back with the excuse that it is not her "business" to narrate the war, Villenoys reports the scene from a distance. Similarly, the fatal message Isabella receives has traveled a great distance. She is given the news of her husband's death by mail. At first, it seems as though Isabella subscribes to the authority of the letter, instantly believing its false information. James Daybell would claim that her acceptance of the news of Henault's death makes sense given the fact that letters were more trusted media of information than oral reports and part of a kind of truth hierarchy that places the personally written letter above rumor (5). However, it is not the letter alone that convinces Isabella, but the fact that the letter is delivered by one of Henault's servants and accompanied by what would seem to be visual proof of his death (243). Interestingly, Henault's servant acts as a private courier in this scene, sent with the letter by Villenoys, who obviously does not use the Post Office to send his news. Henault's servant also testifies to a death he did not witness, and even the picture of Isabella that the servant presents to her as evidence of the death is taken not from Henault's body but his bedside. The servant's delivery also signals Isabella's financial ruin. He gives her "what money [Henault] had, a few jewels, with Isabella's picture that he carried with him and had left in his chamber in the fort of Candia for fear of breaking it in action" (243).[16]

After receiving the news, Isabella isolates herself from her information society, refusing to receive visitors or to respond to messages sent to her. Because she becomes more beautiful each day numerous admirers send her letters, but she does not write back to them. To the public, Isabella's misfortune makes her even more attractive and newsworthy. Her beauty seems to grow exponentially when she suffers, and like a secret that is tempting simply because it is withheld, her physical isolation and refusal to communicate with others are eroticized. Rather than disappear from town discourse as she hopes, she instead becomes an even more famous spectacle, a public figure fixed in the eye of the community.

The scene of Henault's return is staged as a postal delivery and as a covert exchange. He knocks on the door and is described by the narrator as an "old messenger" who "had great news to tell" Isabella (248).[17] He refers to his former wife as if she is a nation-state whose boundaries he must ask permission to pass, offering his wedding ring as "passport" to her, as documentation and proof of identity (248). At first Isabella does not recognize Henault's face, which is hidden under a heavy beard, so he draws attention to his disguise: "Fair creature! Is there no remains of your Henault left in this face of mine, all o'rgrown with hair? Nothing in these eyes, sunk with eight years absence from you and sorrows? Nothing in this shape, bowed with labor and griefs, that can inform you?" (248). Pointing to "remains" of his past self and drawing attention to "sunken" eyes and "bowed" shape, Henault is concerned that his appearance miscommunicates his identity. His return also challenges Isabella's skills of dissemblage. At first she has great difficulty and is unable to "lift her eyes up to consider the face of him whose voice she knew so perfectly well" (248). She finally dissembles successfully, but she cannot psychologically cope with the surprise encounter. She cannot bear the true meaning of this "great news" (248).

Henault returns not simply as himself, a man who has been pronounced dead and returns as if from the dead, but also as a message of Isabella's demise. He is his own documentation of survival and claim for lost property. Unlike Villenoys, who sends the message of death by private postal carrier, Henault returns to deliver his delayed message in person, to make an address to the living. His account of the past seven years reveals that he wrote both Isabella and his father often but received no answers, so the system that initiates Villenoys's happy future with Isabella fails Henault again and again (250).[18] At the same time that he is unable to communicate with any of his relations, the wounded Henault becomes "booty" for the enemy troops and is sold as a slave to a Turkish officer, who sets his ransom too high for Henault to pay (250). He becomes property for profit, transferred from one owner to another through a wartime network that strips prisoners of their inheritance, their identity, and their personal liberty. In this way his position is analogous to that of Isabella.

Up until the climax of the novel, Isabella's only means of adaptation to her community's communication system is to dissemble, to isolate herself, but upon Henault's return she suddenly shifts from a passive to an active participant in that system by continuing the pattern of miscommunication and interception that has dictated the direction of her life. All of Henault's letters to Isabella during his imprisonment are mysteriously lost or intercepted, and after she learns this and "after a thousand convulsions, even worse than death itself, she resolved upon the murder of Henault, as the only means of removing all obstacles to her future happiness" (251). She decides to intercept his message of survival before it reaches the public in order to save herself from the scandal of bigamy. She first plans to cut his throat with a knife, but upon seeing his sleeping face she decides to cover his face with a pillow and smother him because, in Levinas's words, "[t]o be in relation with the other (*autrui*) face to face is to be unable to kill" (9).[19] "At the very moment when my power to kill realizes itself," Levinas explains, "I have not looked at him in the face, I have not encountered his face" (9). When she finally sees him, the sight of his dead face is too much to bear and Isabella becomes guilt-stricken, paranoid, and arguably psychotic:

> But when she had done this dreadful deed, and saw the dead corpse of her once-loved lord lie smiling (as it were) upon her, she fell into a swoon with the horror of the deed, and it had been well for her she had there died; but she revived again and awakened to more and new horrors, she flies all frighted from the chamber and fancies the phantom of her dead lord pursues her; she runs from room to room, and starts and stares, as if she saw him continually before her. Now all that was ever soft and dear to her with him comes into her heart, and she finds he conquers anew, being dead, who could not gain her pity while living. (251)

Behn's decision to represent Isabella's psychological state with Henault's phantom highlights the novel's concern with secret conveyance and multiplicity of messages. Isabella murders Henault before confessing the secret of her adultery. She is haunted by the secret of her sins, by deeds not confessed and as yet undiscovered. Isabella sees several phantoms of her dead husband, so that she is pursued by a *multiplicity* of reminders of her deed. Countering Villenoys's failure to see Henault's body for confirmation of his death, Isabella cannot help but see him dead and, to her horror, after death as well. And unlike the many letters Isabella avoids reading, Henault's ghostly message is impossible to avoid. Though it would seem that her agency will save her reputation from public scrutiny, the imagined phantom foreshadows her eventual fall.

N. Abraham finds that phantoms are "meant to objectify, even if under the guise of individual or collective hallucinations, the gap produced in us by the concealment of some part of a love object's life" (171). The silence of the phantom, Abraham concludes, "refer[s] to the unspeakable" (174). This observation recalls an earlier scene in the novel in which the father's grief is "unspeakable," and thus in a certain sense misfortune is passed down to Isabella through her familial line. The basis of Abraham's essay, in fact, is that the phantom is trans-generational, that it represents a secret passed down from parent to child, until it "fades during its transmission from one genera-tion to the next and [. . .] finally, it disappears" (176). Kittler also considers the phantom but from the perspective of modern media capable of techno-logical reproduction: "Once memories and dreams, the dead and ghosts become technically reproducible, readers and writers no longer need the powers of hallucination." He concludes: "Our realm of the dead has with-drawn from the books in which it resided for so long" (*Gramophone* 10).

Henault's death signals the clash of the old and the new. The language before the murder relies on images of aging: an "old messenger," his beard makes visual the passing of time, his eyes are "sunk with eight years absence," and he walks bent over, like an old man (248). After Isabella smothers him, faints, and recovers, however, the narrator's account is unmistakably con-cerned with the new: she sees "more and new horrors" everywhere she looks, she suddenly remembers her love for him, and he "conquers anew" (251). Even the phantom, whom she fears pursues her from behind, is instead "con-tinually before her" (251). On an obvious level, the scene contradicts the narrator's earlier assertion that Isabella "could not recall her love, for love like reputation once fled never returns more" (249). The scene's contrast of the present and past also, however, reiterates the conflict between news and the vow; news is a communication act concerned most with the near past, with things that have *just* happened, and bound only by the present, while the vow continues over a long period of time. Henault's suffocation, then, marks the end of her vow to him. The developing system of instantaneous and simultaneous message delivery is too much for the vow—as only one com-munication act among others, it is smothered by the countless new messages circulating in its network.

Unlike the first knock on the door by Henault, which shifts the *History* into bizarre, highly psychological narrative, Villenoys's knock is one with "authority" that seems at first to bring her back to reality (251).[20] Isabella cannot escape the ceaseless return of the fatal message. Villenoys takes the news of Henault's survival with surprisingly little reaction, and he appears to believe Isabella when she dishonestly claims that Henault died naturally after she confessed her remarriage.[21] The couple decides to dump Henault's body in the river as a "last office for the dead," and Villenoys slings the body over his shoulder, prepared to depart for delivery and get rid of the old messenger once and for all (253).

Isabella's murder of Villenoys marks the second moment in the narrative when her behavior is active rather than merely reactive and, perhaps more importantly, when she successfully conceals her intent as well as her response. As Villenoys stands with the body wrapped in a sack and thrown over his shoulder, Isabella, pretending to sew the sack closed, actually sews it to Vil-lenoy's collar "without him perceiving it" (254). Her language also changes, and she issues a rare command to her husband to "be sure you give him a good swing, lest the sack should hang on any thing at the side of the bridge and not fall into the stream" (254). Villenoys responds, in a defensively authoritative tone, "I'll warrant you, I know how to secure his falling" (254). He leaves to deliver Henault's body, carrying the "package" to the bridge. When he throws the body over into the stream, the weight of the bundle pulls him over also. The private courier, tied to his message, dies with the delivery of the dead, and Isabella kills both husbands in what must be less than an hour.[22]

No scholar has yet explained why Isabella murders Villenoys. Depending upon how one reads the battle scene, however, Villenoys may actually be the villain in the novel and Isabella the victim who cannot see his plotting until she decides to murder him, whose fate has nothing to do with broken vows but with his secret plan to conquer her. If upon Henault's return she suddenly realizes his death was purposely misreported and that her marriage to Villenoys all part of a plan Villenoys himself devised, her quick decision makes more sense. She may indeed realize that she has been ambushed. Looking back to the battle scene, additional evidence of Villenoys's plan surfaces. Villenoys, the narrator points out, led the men to the battlefield the day of Henault's alleged death, and Henault is the only man named as fallen during the battle. When Villenoys first visits Isabella, he relates "every circumstance of Henault's death" even though he did not know every circumstance (245). All of Henault's letters after his reported death mysteriously disappear in the narrative, and one speculation could be that they were intercepted by Villenoys, who did not want them to reach her.

By killing her husbands, Isabella destroys the secret of her transgressions. In this way her response is not only murder, but also erasure. After the murders, Isabella waits for news but at first hears none. Once the bodies are discovered, however, reports of the murders circulate back and forth in the small town. After "news was brought that two men were found dead," the narrative is flooded with messages. "News was brought in," "'twas reported," a messenger "ran home with the news," and Maria enters, "weeping with the news" of the "fatal truth" (254–255). For the first time, Isabella knows the meaning of the message before it reaches her, before it even becomes a message. For the first time, Isabella makes her own news.[23] Her surprising decision is her final attempt to disconnect herself from the two modes of discourse that have controlled her life throughout the narrative. She ends the timeline of her vows to both husbands and foresees "the greatest assaults of fate" because she becomes the assailant (222).

Like lost virginity or love, a message sent into circulation can never return as it first was. Readers will inevitably misinterpret the meaning of a message once it is lifted out of its original context, and their distortions of the message redefine the subject, tarnish reputation, and redirect the transmission of social and familial rewards, such as inheritance. As Isabella begins to discover, she can only temporarily interrupt the circulation of discourse. She smothers her first husband in order to secure her secret, and she drowns the second to keep the secret from being passed on. What she does not anticipate, however, is that her information society relies upon a multiplicity and simultaneity of message delivery that does not break down when a single pathway is interrupted.

As a murderer, Isabella creates a news event, yet her control is only momentary. Before he returned to find her, Henault wrote his name and address on a piece of paper, which he gave to a new friend and fellow prisoner of war. The friend, identified only as a French colleague, reaches Henault's home after the murders. Throughout Behn's *History* messages are misreported, lost, unanswered, and postponed, and this marks the first time that a note—the content of which is actually an address—arrives on time, at its intended destination, unchanged. The note is also significant because it links Henault to his original property, though the house and possessions he finds on his return are "infinitely more magnificent than he had left 'em," because they no longer belong to him (250). Literally an address to the living, the note's appearance begins a chain of events that finally leads to Isabella's confession and execution.[24] Confused, the Frenchman, thinking he has failed as private courier, leaves the house and enters town, where he hears about the recent murders and requests the bodies be exhumed. In Kittler's words, Henault's writing "stores the fact of [his] authorization" (*Gramophone* 7). As with the scandal of the Popish Plot, private written communication in the *History* becomes public and prompts the investigation of a violent crime, and it reminds others of the consequences of broken promises.

Immediately upon the discovery of Henault's identity, Isabella "delivers herself" to the magistrate of justice and confesses her crimes. The narrator speaks in global terms, remarking that the "whole world stood amazed" at her confession of the murders. The last news Isabella hears is that she is sentenced to lose her head (257). From that point on she warns those who visit her never to break a vow, seemingly subscribing to the traditions of authority that confined her, transforming herself into a negative example, transmitting her own message to fellow widows. Citizens like Isabella are condemned by an existing "legally constituted authority" that does not recognize the incompatibility of discourses operating within its community ("Spectacular" 83).[25]

Within the context of the contemporary communication systems that drive the plot, Isabella's execution can be read as the final postal delivery in the novel. Prepared for death, she delivers a thirty-minute speech to her audience from behind a mourning veil about the importance of keeping vows, but the details of that speech are not transcribed by the narrator, who only remarks that "it was as amazing to hear her as it was to behold her" (257).[26] Readers are informed that the speech is "eloquent," but its message, not passed on in the text, goes no further than the crowd who gathers to watch her. Like her vow to God and her two marriages, Isabella's death is public, but because she covers her face she hides her expressions from the audience, creating a sense of privacy for herself and consequently intensifying the crowd's interest, or "wonder," in her (257). Immediately before she is decapitated, however, she lifts her veil like the flap of an envelope. A dead letter in her life, misdirected and lost in a system that promises privacy yet is vulnerable to manipulation by others, she finally confronts the public by delivering herself before them.

Through local news, gossip, and letters that travel within an expanding global network, the *History* builds a plot from a sequence of correspondences that conceal and disclose characters' identities and that parallel disruptions in inheritance networks. The last of the de Valerie line, Isabella leaves no property or wealth behind her. The de Valerie birthright is apparently transferred to the Church, and Villenoys's substantial wealth and property is passed on to unknown hands since, childless, he is also the last of his bloodline. Meant to be a final statement to which the crowd cannot respond, her death seems to halt the circulation of the town discourse of which she has always been the main topic. Yet because her story goes on to be archived in Iper's records, and because that story is retold by the *History's* narrator, Isabella remains part of a permanent circulating discourse.

In her work on epistolary fiction written by eighteenth-century French and British women, April Alliston argues that "fictions of women's correspondence," as she calls them, are linked by the plot of inheritance. She defines the plot of inheritance in both familial and textual terms. Female characters in the epistolary fiction Alliston describes, denied inheritance because of the patriarchal system of transmitting property and wealth, create a system of textual inheritance through written correspondence with other women. Though letters drive its plot, Behn's *History* is not an epistolary fiction, nor is there any correspondence between female characters. On the contrary, the only letters sent between or by women—Isabella's messages to her aunt, for example, or her messages to male characters like Villenoys—are never read or answered. Behn's parallel treatment of inheritance and communication systems suggests that textual correspondence, at least as it takes place through the postal system that still very much depends upon private couriers, is not necessarily liberating but yet another medium through which female behavior is objectified and controlled.

Chapter Three

Suffocation by Information: Collectivity and the Secretary in Swift's *A Tale of a Tub*

> Whoever hath an ambition to be heard in a crowd must press, and squeeze, and thrust, and climb, with indefatigable pains, till he has exalted himself to a certain degree of altitude above them. Now, in all assemblies though you wedge them ever so close, we may observe this peculiar property that over their heads there is room enough, but how to reach it is the difficult point, it being as hard to get quit of *number* as of *hell*. (25)

It is no secret that the crowd Jonathan Swift's narrator describes in the introduction to *A Tale of a Tub* is a metaphor for his community's print culture.[1] Kenneth Craven, in the first study to engage thoroughly with the *Tale's* critique of rational scientific systems in terms of information multiplicity, notes the narrator's anxieties about his era's "enormous outpouring of processed information" (7). Similarly, Marilyn Francus argues that "he is disturbed by the *quantity* of language, not by its quality," and Warren Montag agrees that "it is full space not empty space that frightens him" (57, 101).[2] While Craven, Francus, and Montag provide valuable insight into the *Tale's* criticism of multiplicity and scientific empiricism, they may underestimate the significance of the text's consideration of what we today call *information,* a term that appears at an important moment in the *Tale*.[3] Moreover, the narrator's commentary on the emergence of secretarial authorship has gone largely unnoticed, though Swift may have started the *Tale* when he served as personal secretary for Sir William Temple (Ellis 72). The *Tale's* structure draws the reader into an experiment in literacy reform.

Swift's narrator appears to conclude that the best way to be heard in the crowd is to rise above it, to emerge as an individual and speak from an elevated position. As further examination of the intertwined narrative of allegory and digression in the *Tale* reveals, however, elevation is unattainable for two reasons. First, the crowd operates on the problematic belief in universal accessibility, of the inalienable right of all citizens to receive and to deliver information. Like twentieth-century citizens, Craven finds, Swift's crowd longs for information that is "instantaneously accessible to the specialist and to the public" (9). Secondly, the crowd is unable to organize its members, so that they collaborate with rather than compete against each another to initiate a collective effort.[4] It is not multiplicity that is harmful but the inability of the group to systematize its conversation and learn habits of literacy necessary to communicate .effectively. "Number," then, while not a problem in itself, makes obvious the society's failure to organize itself. Visually, the crowd, gathered together in a central location, appears unified. Audibly, however, the voices of the crowd's members are cacophonous. They do not speak to one another but over one another, competing for silent moments during which their voices can be heard by the others. The crowd exhibits what Lèvy describes as the "deliberate organization of ignorance," and it challenges Ong's claim that sight is a "dissecting sense" and sound a "unifying sense" (*Collective* 14, Ong 72).

While at first a symbol of the failure of modern information systems to enable citizens to communicate with each other, the crowd changes its metaphorical meaning over the course of the work. By the end, it becomes a metaphor for the collectively constructed text, a collaborative type of writing that confuses the distinction between author and reader and in which the number of producers seems excessive. In a sense, mass media is revised as multimedia. Reflective of his methods of organizing information in his *Tale,* the narrator participates in what Lèvy would call a virtualization of the text, exposing the technological innovation that makes the text accessible to its readers. Structurally, he considers the consequences of collection as a strategy for managing multiple texts and authors. Rhetorically, he examines metaphors commonly used to characterize communication in terms of vertical and organic depth and proposes a new visual trope that (dis)organizes information in knots. In its innovative narrative structure, paratext, and playful awareness of the implications of metaphors used to describe communication, the *Tale* represents a secretarial model of organization that successfully negotiates secrecy and publicity to communicate with its reader.[5] To date, attention to Swift's critique of information has focused on his relationship with the public sphere and public opinion. David Oakleaf, for example, notes the influence of public institutions, like clubs and the bookselling business, on Swift, categorizing these systems as "in brief, everything associated with the dissemination and social reception of 'information,' especially its public debate" (43). Yet no thorough study of Swift and information has yet been developed, excepting Craven's *Jonathan Swift and the Millenium of Madness* (1992), upon which this chapter builds.

Scholars of the *Tale* have generally agreed that the narrator represents and demonstrates a degenerate literary culture against which Swift satirically aligns himself. Whether labeled a hack writer, a "loony smartaleck," a "buffoon," a "toady," a "madman," or all of these personas combined, as John Traugott describes, the speaker has been accepted by scholars as the modern enemy of those, like Swift, who are nostalgic for the ancients (152). What has gone unnoticed, however, is that the narrator identifies himself not as an author but as a secretary, a position that Swift himself held in the service of Temple. Though many scholars, such as Ian Higgins, mention that Swift wrote the *Tale* while serving as Temple's secretary, most have not explored how that position may have affected the *Tale*'s physical structure. The only influence usually mentioned is that the *Tale* defends Temple's *Upon Ancient and Modern Learning* (1690) against William Wotton's *Reflections Upon Ancient and Modern Learning* (1694) (Mueller 204). Carole Fabricant acknowledges that the experience may have been "creatively productive" but focuses more on the fact that the position did not lead to any career advancement for the author (50). Brean Hammond finds a list of books Swift read during his employment but does not focus on the employment itself, using the book list to prove that Swift was an "omnivorous reader, not to say a polymath" (73). David Deeming, who makes more of Swift and Temple's working relationship in terms of literary production, still does not consider the influence of Swift's responsibilities as secretary, of what he actually did each day in his employment and how his secretarial writing may have changed his literary strategies. When Higgins mentions the physical fragmentation of the *Tale,* he likens it to Temple's fragmented take on the ancient/modern debate (27).

Though it is impossible to identify moments in the *Tale* when Swift speaks through the narrator as himself or, conversely, when he is ridiculing the narrator, the narrator's professional identity as secretary suggests that the two figures have more in common with one another than critics have acknowledged.[6] Joseph McMinn adds that Swift saw himself "as a kind of literary public servant" more so than as a career writer for profit (19). Swift certainly critiques the modernization of communication, like Behn and Defoe, yet he stages a plan of reform as the innovation of a seemingly mindless—though admittedly creative—secretary. With the narrator as his agent, Swift is able to stage a multi-dimensional satirical portrayal of modern information systems and, without losing stride, double back to propose a solution that capitalizes upon rather than abolishes the ignorance that characterizes contemporary hack culture. By the end, the narrator becomes an instrument, a medium of communication, with and through which the satirist can address and change the progress of his contemporary technological environment.[7] What might be most interesting about the catalog Hammond discovers is that Swift felt compelled to make a list of literary influences in the first place. He found value in listing and thus making visible and organized the history of his reading.[8]

The collective scriptural metaphor of the coat, worn by each of the father's sons in the allegory of Peter, Jack, and Martin, highlights the emergence of the knot as an alternative to the multi-layered plane of bodily flesh and organ. As Allen Reddick finds, the body is a metaphorical dead-end for Swift, a "rhetoric of death" (161).[9] This substitute organizational pattern, in turn, marks an early historical understanding of the material and communicative aspects of knowing, or *information* in today's vocabulary, that media theorists have assumed did not happen before the mid-nineteenth century. Kittler, for example, sees the late nineteenth century as the beginning of a new type of reading, which he calls "automatic," during which a reader aims for speed rather than understanding, and a writer strives to make reading as fast and easy as possible through shorter words and changes in the positioning of text (*Discourse* 223–6). The narrator's discussion of index reading, however, proves that automatic reading is a concern much earlier than the twentieth century, and that authors like Swift were in very self-conscious ways already trying to figure out how to counter this tendency, playing with the appearance of words and rethinking the organization of their narratives.[10] One cannot even make the argument that twentieth-century automatic reading is unique because of its technological impetuses; for example, that telegraph, telephone, and typewriter create more urgent reading environments because citizens must read faster in order to keep up with the messages coming through the wires or pages typed with unprecedented speed. At the end of *A Discourse Concerning the Mechanical Operation of the Spirit* (1704), Swift's narrator apologizes for concluding hastily, explaining that "the post is just going, which forces me in great haste to conclude" (141). Every information system challenges users to adapt to a new pace, changing temporal relations between the everyday and the technological.

Throughout the *Tale,* the narrator exhibits increasing anxieties that multiplicity in the print market will inevitably lead to intellectual exhaustion. He is most concerned with the large number of authors in his community who write, publish, and circulate texts with whirlwind speed. "[T]he number of writers must needs have increased accordingly, and to a pitch that has made it of absolute necessity for them to interfere continually with each other," he writes in "A Digression in Praise of Digressions" (70). He fears that with so many writers, there will be nothing left to write: "there is not at this present a sufficient quantity of new matter left in nature to furnish and adorn any one particular subject to the extent of a volume" (70). Like an army that leaves the area in which it camps "barren and dry, affording no sustenance but clouds of dust," literary overpopulation exhausts knowledge (70).

The narrator suggests that the solution to the problem of textual surplus is simple: authors should write without digression, communicating only that information they set out to communicate (69).[11] What he finds has happened instead, however, is that writers have turned to collections, or "large indexes, and little compendiums," as alternatives to original thought, gathering together random observations in lists and copying phrases from other texts in commonplace books. Creative genius has given way to organizational manipulation. Ong discusses the appeal of indexes and compendiums as aesthetic objects with organizational rather than intellectual appeal, noting that indexes actually "seem to have been valued at times for their beauty and mystery" instead of for their usefulness (124). He believes that though indexes are supposed to help a reader work more efficiently through books or volume of books, they are actually counterproductive, distracting readers' attention away from the content of the work toward the visual image before them. Words and phrases, which are excerpted from the body of the text and copied into the index for quick reference, lose their contextual meaning and become "mysterious," creating meaning only in their spatial relationships with other decontextualized words and phrases on the page. "Alphabetic indexes," Ong concludes, "show strikingly the disengagement of words from discourse and their embedding in typographic space" (124).

Swift's narrator presents his own text as an organizational wonder, even going so far as to invite his readers to reorganize it as they see fit: "I do here impower him to remove it into any other corner he please" (72). Like an index, the *Tale* as a whole is a typographical marvel. Structurally, it combines a sequence of digressions in chapter and footnote form, which appear as though they can be rearranged without affecting meaning. Interspersed throughout the work, the digressions pull readers continually away from the more traditional linear narrative of the religious allegory. Indeed, a digression is a thought out of context, at once fascinating and distracting.

The narrator quickly abandons his discussion of writers to focus on the way in which the reading habits of his time have changed as a result of multiplicity. The natural consequence is that readers feel that they have to read as much as they physically can; the more there is to read, the faster they must work to cover all the material. He focuses on two particular strategies that his contemporaries have adopted in order to avoid "the fatigue of reading or of thinking" (70). First, some familiarize themselves with titles, so that they can drop references to several books into conversations. More ambitious readers take a further step and peruse a book's index.[12] The narrator compares this to "get[ting] in by the back door" and "attacking in the rear," likening index reading to cheating (70). Though he does not make the point explicitly, his metaphor also reflects an increasingly common attitude among readers that they are always behind, that they must find shortcuts to keep up with authors. Literacy, as the *Tale* depicts it, is a high-stakes battlefield in which readers struggle to defend themselves against a quicker, larger enemy. Though the narrator intends to depict readers on the offensive, "flinging" texts like dead fish, he actually portrays a rather defenseless audience assaulted by texts, coping any way it can (70).

The consequences of textual multiplicity and excessive readerly consumption and exhaustion are dramatic: the narrator fears the inevitable extinction of all texts, exemplified in his dedication to Prince Posterity. The dedication to Posterity takes public anxiety about the disappearance of documents as its sole object, and the narrator laments that the Prince's governor has attempted to persuade him that "our age is almost wholly illiterate, and has hardly produced one writer upon any subject" (14). While at first glance it seems that the footnote writer is absolutely correct and that the narrator is simply ridiculing his contemporary writers' tendency to appeal to posterity in a way that they should "conceal and be ashamed of," the epistle dedicatory also provides an important commentary on literacy (14). Prince Posterity represents the ultimate consequence of a society of literate citizens that never stops reading, that consumes without discrimination. Representing the other extreme, the Prince reads nothing because his governor, Time, restricts him from perusing anything before it disappears: "The originals were posted fresh upon all gates and corners of the streets but, returning in a very few hours to take a review, they were all torn down, and fresh ones in their places" (16). The proliferation of texts after the 1695 lapse of the Licensing Act, which had restricted any new printers from setting up shop, saturates the print market to such an extent that the narrator fears textual overpopulation will lead to the inevitable annihilation of the communication system on which it relies.[13]

Literacy, for Swift's narrator, is more than simply knowing how to read and write: it is also learning how to *stop* reading, how to choose between those texts worth reading and those that are a waste of time. As his governor convinces the Prince, the "age is almost wholly illiterate, and has hardly produced one writer upon any subject" (14). Indeed, it has not produced one but many; the well-read citizen in the narrator's view is not one who has read much but who has selected his texts carefully enough to have read little. As evidenced by the tone of this passage, Swift mistrusts such scholarly practices and the reasoning that overabundance should necessarily lead to careless literacy. At the same time, however, the narrator's perspective, though it may be naïve, is inviting. The narrator rages that Time's "inveterate malice is such to the writings of our age that of several thousands produced yearly from this renowned city, before the next revolution of the sun there is not one to be heard of" (15). Time, he accuses, has destroyed the evidence that the present age has produced any piece of writing whatsoever. He predicts that the Governor will himself ask for proof of the documents' past existence, asking "Who has mislaid them? Are they sunk in the abyss of things? [. . .] Who has annihilated them? Were they drowned by purges, or martyred by pipes?" (15). He reasons that texts, because they are physical objects, cannot simply disappear into thin air and cease to exist unless some force, human or otherwise, destroys them. Replacement, he argues, is not necessarily death: "Books, like men their authors, have no more than one way of coming into the world, but there are ten thousand to go out of it and return no more" (17). The narrator's anxieties about multiplicity center on extinction.[14]

One answer the narrator provides for Governor Time's questions about what happens to all of the texts that are replaced by others "before the next revolution of the sun" is that they are disassembled and reassembled, that they do not necessarily disappear but are mutilated beyond recognition. He reports that "some [Time] flays alive; others he tears limb from limb," and that others "die of a languishing consumption" (15). To preserve a text for posterity's sake, then, is necessarily to deny the text its present: "what I am going to say is literally true this minute I am writing," the narrator stresses, but "[w]hat revolutions may happen before it shall be ready for your perusal, I can by no means warrant" (17). On the one hand, editors and printers stand between the text written by the author and perused by the reader. On the other hand, commentators and critics footnote and annotate, add and subtract from the text, cutting it up in ways that they think will make it last longer or, if they disagree with its content, ensure that it will not survive to influence readers. The original text is the individual in the crowd, silenced when it is "pressed" by those in the business of deciding what will and will not be read. The text does not survive in its original form but is consumed by its intertextuality.

Swift's *Tale* reminds readers of a significant development in the early eighteenth century that today characterizes multimedia: copied and excerpted, the original text may never be read. Instead, readers encounter a collectively constructed text that has been modified by editors and commentators after the manuscript leaves the author's hands or, as the narrator notes, they read texts that are compilations of multiple originals, collections that splice together parts of originals to form a new work that resembles the gaudy coats of Peter, Martin, and Jack, the protagonists of the *Tale's* religious allegory. The more time between the first writing and the moment a reader encounters the published text, the more multiplicity it will exhibit: "if his papers had been a long time out of his possession, they must have still undergone more severe corrections" (5).

The first step toward solving the apparent problem of the individual silenced by the crowd, the narrator reveals, is to examine whether collections—of people or of texts—are as stifling as they at first seem. From the epistle dedicatory to Prince Posterity to the end of the last section of the *Tale,* the narrator will return again and again to the idea of collection, struggling to determine whether collecting is always necessarily destructive or if, with more practice and experimentation, it can be harnessed to create a more effective communication system that turns the problems of multiplicity into advantages. Twentieth-century media theorists, such as Lèvy, have determined that the modern digital age is driven to answer this basic question above all others. In his analysis of multiplicity and the virtual, he determines that virtualization, which he defines as the new reality that results when citizens redefine a problem and solution in such a way that the very concepts of inside and outside and private and public are called into question, is often mistakenly thought of as a loss, a disappearance, or a fake (*Becoming* 94, 1). On the contrary, the virtual is dynamic and immaterial, not a replica of reality but an act of reorganization that occurs when unprecedented problems force citizens to develop alternative systems to live by. In this way, collections are virtual texts—the first of three categories Lèvy delineates when he defines the virtual in terms of texts, bodies, and economies. Any act of reading is necessarily involved in virtualization, he argues, when readers set out to "solve" the meaning of a text like the *Tale* by "undoing" it (47). Like Swift's narrator, Lèvy agrees that the dissection of the text is the reverse of reading, is *not* reading, by means of decontextualization (47).

Readers, overwhelmed by textual surplus, turn to collecting as a means of containment. To minimize the burdens of reading, they select passages and phrases from original texts and assemble them to create single, portable compendia. They confront mass production by becoming producers, and the texts they produce, in turn, appear to repeat the problem of multiplicity on a smaller scale. Like the print market as a whole, a single text like the *Tale* may host an unruly mob of contributors, juxtaposing pieces of original text with little if any transition or connection between them except spatial positioning, forcing authors to speak over one another. Although the *Tale* does not present itself as a collection of this nature, the narrator does repeatedly admit that he collects material for his narrative from "indefatigable reading" (92).[15] At the same time, he also emphasizes the presence of other voices that contribute to the *Tale*, textually or contextually. In the opening apology, the author speaks directly against his critics, bringing their commentary into the narrative and, in the process, revealing a complex underlying network of producers involved in the writing and publication of his book. He openly accuses "those who had the papers in their power" of omitting material that appeared in his original manuscript, and he responds to comments made by the bookseller to the reader, a document that is included as part of the *Tale's* paratext (4). Throughout the work, authors, booksellers, and footnote writers comment on one another's points, agreeing and disagreeing about changing the text's narrative structure (making it more complex) and physical shape (making it longer and thicker).

If reading has become an enterprise of collectors and writing becomes the compilation of other works already written, then the distinction between reading and writing is difficult to pinpoint. One consequence of textual multiplicity that particularly bothers the narrator is the apparent transformation of readers into writers. Readers, the narrator fears, look to original texts not for meaning or knowledge but merely for material to copy into their own books. They also interrupt other texts by adding their own versions, modifications, and commentaries. In this way, readers determine the direction of the narrative and, though the narrator does not note it, they create new knowledge in an interactive way. Ong attributes this kind of authorial shift to print, but he does not emphasize the reader's more privileged position as Swift does: "With the control of information and memory brought about by writing and, more intensely, by print, you do not need a hero in the old sense to mobilize knowledge in story form" (71). Ong does not explain exactly who is in "control of information and memory" after print. In Swift's *Tale*, however, all of the participants in the text's production and reception—the author, printer, commentator, and reader—share the responsibility of shaping the narrative. The identity of Ong's "hero" who "mobilizes knowledge" is the storyteller who travels from town to town, physically moving stories and their lessons.[16]

Shedding his title of writer and "modern author," the narrator instead calls himself a secretary. Secretaries, the first bureaucratic officers whose exclusive duty was information management, were integral to the development of seventeenth- and eighteenth-century communication systems. Whether transcribing another's letter, writing on behalf of an employer like Temple, or intercepting correspondence in the interest of national security, secretaries complicated the distinction between writing and reading on a daily basis. They organized new narratives from parts of original texts, assembled complete narratives from information given by multiple writers, and changed the course of an unfolding story by inserting themselves, as simultaneous readers and writers, in the ongoing correspondence. Like Ong's hero, they "mobilize[d] knowledge," yet they did so by managing reading and writing as simultaneous and inseparable activities (59).

Peter, Martin, and Jack, the protagonists of the narrator's allegorical history of Catholicism, Anglicanism, and "radical personal belief," demonstrate the narrator's secretarial habits, constantly shaping and recreating their coats even though they are explicitly directed by their father to wear and maintain them in their original design (Ross and Woolley x). Their father identifies them only as readers, asking them to familiarize themselves with his "full instructions in every particular" (34). Instead, when they see the new fashion of shoulder knots, they immediately begin to read his instructions with the intent of changing rather than preserving the originals. As Judith C. Mueller supports, each brother demonstrates a different style of reading and interpreting scripture (210). By representing scripture as a coat, the narrator can give visible form to the history of Biblical interpretation. Readers can see interpretive liberties as the surface of the coat, physical modifications that accumulate over time. The result is a coat that externalizes its reading, an eclectic fashion statement that records its textual evolution: "there was hardly a thread of the original coat to be seen, but an infinite quantity of *lace* and *ribbons,* and *fringe,* and *embroidery,* and *points*" (65). Because previous accessories are not removed before new fashions are added, the coats become collections of past and present readings. They also become compilations of multiple authors' textual inventions. When a "certain lord came just from Paris with fifty yards of gold lace upon his coat," the brothers copy what they see onto their own coats (39). Multiplicity on the "micro-coat" level then, is present both as multiple authorship and as the visible association and juxtaposition of different parts of the interpretive process (36).

Through the metaphor of the coats, the narrator is able to emphasize the collective nature of scripture. Collaboratively authored, the Old and New Testaments juxtapose voices and make public the revision of the Word. That there are separate coats in the *Tale,* and not a single one shared by the three brothers, further stresses the narrator's point that there are also multiple versions of scripture, each modified by individual readers. The fundamental question, then, is how readers can communicate with one another if they each interpret, and in the process rewrite, the text differently. Neither the individual pressed in the crowd nor the text lost among a whirlwind of other printed texts poses problems that are altogether new. Looking to the history of religious reform, Swift locates the dilemmas of his media culture within the broader contexts of multiplicity; the mass productive possibilities of print make the potential erasure or forgetting of scriptural teachings an even more urgent problem than before. Communication between Peter, Martin, and Jack soon breaks down when they begin to read differently and create their own versions of their father's instructions. The coats' visible evolution, their exteriorization of the reading and revision process, is an important part of the narrator's growing realization that scripture is itself a collection, a compilation of different works juxtaposing different authorial voices.

Just as the coats give visible form to the history of scriptural interpretation, so too does the *Tale* lay bare its evolution as document. On the syntactical level, the narrator often changes his mind in mid-sentence, presenting both the original thought and the substitution simultaneously. Describing the *History of Reynard the Fox*, for example, he asserts that he does not "think any of the learned will dispute that famous treatise to be a complete body of civil knowledge and the revelation, or rather the apocalypse, of all State Arcana" (31). "Or rather" and "that is to say" phrases, which signal moments of conscious revision, abound in the *Tale* (31, 73). Francus observes that the narrator creates the illusion that he is "moving between personae, ideas, or languages," by leaving behind remnants of discarded voices, thoughts, and words (51). In one short passage, wisdom begins as a "a fox" but then is metaphorically revised as "a cheese," "a sack-posset," "a hen," and "a nut" (30–1). In a critique of the conventions of preface writing, the narrator describes the inspirations for writing commonly related by authors in their prefaces:

> If it were not for a rainy day, a drunken vigil, a fit of the spleen, a course of the physic, a sleepy Sunday, an ill run at dice, a long tailor's bill, a beggar's purse, a factious head, a hot sun, costive diet, want of books, and a just contempt of learning, [. . .] I doubt the number of authors and of writings would dwindle away to a degree most woeful to behold.
> (88)

These lists are organized horizontally within a line of prose, yet they also create the impression of vertical movement, proceeding deeper through layers of meaning until readers cannot remember the context of what they are read-ing. Francus argues that the narrator's lists of metaphors and images frustrate readers' attempts to find meaning in the *Tale:* "The rapid sequencing of lay-ered images usually prohibits the development of the argument that it intends to substantiate because the evidence cannot be satisfactorily summed up, and consequently, it cannot establish a basis for further advocacy or analysis" (91). Like hypertext, these phrases also link readers to other writ-ings, in this case to past prefaces that describe such motives.

The structure of the *Tale* makes readers more aware of their physical movement through the narrative. For example, the reader is often invited to digress with the narrator, sometimes moving to new sections and sometimes switching within sections. "I now happily resume my subject, to the infinite satisfaction both of the reader and the author," the narrator writes before his transition to third installment of the allegory of Peter, Martin, and Jack. Kit-tler would call this type of syntactical and structural movement a system of "virtual substitutes" in which words and ideas are "endlessly further inscribed and denied" (*Discourse* 12–13). Describing his career as a secretary, an office that provides and denies information on a daily basis, the narrator acknowl-edges that he has worked hard "to give the learned reader an idea as well as a taste of what the whole work is likely to produce" (32). Francus notes that the *Tale* "is a literature of process rather than product" (51). Moreover, the narrator also sees his *Tale* not as product but as producer; it is a text eternally under revision because how and what it means changes as it is read. As the narrator's description of his secretarial career acknowledges, it is also a work that "is likely to produce" something else (32). The narrator's interests in col-lecting suggest he intends the *Tale* to produce other texts, whether attacks by critics, analyses by scholars, or compilations by collectors.

To twenty-first century readers, the narrator's method of shaping a discourse by displaying his mental processes of association resembles hyper-text, which is also code in the guise of intelligible text.[17] Lèvy sees hypertext as the "result of a series of decisions" and claims that in "hypertext every act of reading is an act of writing" (*Becoming* 55, 59). For Lèvy, however, this transformation does not signal the end of writing but the "technological vir-tualization and exteriorization of the reading process" (63). Hypertext is not the first kind of writing that makes visible the direction or progress of a writer's thoughts and decisions, nor is it the first to allow readers to move so freely through texts, shaping the narrative through physical participation in the ordering and association of events. Obviously, I am not claiming that the relationships between writer and text and reader and text are exactly the same in the *Tale* and on the internet, but rather that the "virtualization and exteriorization of the reading process" that Lèvy describes is not a phenomenon only of the digital age.

The narrator's sudden narrative decisions and lists of metaphors on the sentence level, and his visible navigation through digression on the structural level, are further highlighted by the imagery of interiority and exteriority that dominates the *Tale*. As critics such as Montag have noted, the narrator relies upon the language of insides and outsides, presenting one image after another that involves consumption, excretion, and dissection.[18] One of Swift's main projects, after all, is to "display by incision" the systems of religion and learning that are targets of his satire (31). A solution for the communication problem that burdens the group gathered at the beginning of the introduction suggests that members of the crowd lie horizontally with their mouths agape so that they can more easily consume the words of orators (28). He writes often of reading as appetite and as nausea, as filling up and emptying out. The mind, the body, and the page are spaces made uncomfortable by the rapid passage of words and ideas from the outside to the inside and back out again. Reading is likened to "a depraved and *debauched appetite*" that is at once ravenous for more texts and "too long nauseated with endless repetitions upon every subject" (69, 2). Dreaming of a complete and portable volume of all the world's knowledge, he recites the directions he finds in an anonymous author. Although the narrator categorizes all readers as either title or index learners, the anonymous author he quotes proposes yet another possible shortcut, a chemical elixir, for those who wish to master texts with minimum effort:

> You take fair correct copies, well bound in calf-skin, and lettered at the back, of all modern bodies of arts and sciences whatsoever, and in what language you please [. . .] Then you begin your Catholic treatise, taking every morning fasting (first shaking the vial) three drops of this elixir, snuffing it strongly up your nose. It will dilate itself about the brain (where there is any) in fourteen minutes, and you immediately perceive in your hand an infinite number of abstracts, summaries, compendiums, extracts, collections, medullas, excerpta quædams, florilegias, and the like, all disposed into great order, and reducible upon paper. (60–1)

Craven takes note of the narrator's treatment of "information in the brain and drugs in the body" as parallel addictions in this passage, pointing out that alchemical imagery proves that universal access operates like a hallucinatory drug, that it is an illusion (10). "This bootless fantasy has been subliminally implanted both in modern minds and in their information systems,"

Craven accurately states, and the *Tale* "devalues the millennial myth as hastening our inevitable mortality, tyranny, madness, and deconstruction" (10). In the passage Swift's narrator also critiques the language of interiorization and exteriorization, the metaphors of consumption that are used rhetorically to characterize and describe information and its multiplicity.

In the narrator's description of the elixir, readers do not read; they merely ingest texts in their material forms and then magically see the organizational properties outlined before them. By simply viewing in gestalt the association of one idea with another, readers can understand texts without reading them. Eisenstein points out that there is a difference between "literacy and habitual book reading" and that "learning to read is different [from] learning by reading" (65). The narrator shows that a distinction also exists between learning by reading and learning by *not* reading (65). The promise of universal access depends upon rhetoric that uses temporal and spatial generalizations that oversimplify knowledge. Describing information as the surface of the hand, for example, reduces it to the status of a lesser knowledge, while describing it as a liquid elixir, a hallucinatory drug, condemns it as a medium of distortion rather than promotes it as a medium of instruction and understanding.

Critically, there is debate amongst scholars about whether Swift sees surface information positively or negatively. Mueller, for example, believes that Swift promotes the superficial rather than condemns it, though she admits that "[n]either surface wisdom nor depth proves to be a completely acceptable means of knowing (211). "If there is a third alternative," she concludes, "Swift never makes it clear" (212). Unlike Mueller, Blanchard sees in the *Tale* a "distrust in the surfaces of things" (65). Obviously, Swift's commentary on the semantics of information is part of his satire on the rationality of contemporary scriptural interpretation. Boyle finds that for Swift, "a religiously divisive debate over the physical events of the Eucharist has all the rational merit of an argument about, for example, the physical modes of communication between Homer and his muse" (115). Boyle summarizes this critique as Swift's challenge to "materialist discourse" (115). Yet even Swift would probably admit that within the context of information, the material and bodily provide a language, albeit one that often falls short, with which to discuss changes in the cultural influences of communication systems.

The elixir allows its drinker to know texts without reading them or even understanding the languages in which they are written. In the same way, information is at once decontextualized and ultimately dependent upon context to communicate meaning. It is simultaneously organic bodily waste, knowledge undigested and left behind, and a synthetic prescription for revelation, knowledge neurologically mobilized and perceptively magnified. Only in the twenty-first century, Thurtle and Mitchell find, have theorists realized that "bodies and information continually graft themselves onto one another in a number of different cultural domains" (1). Yet Swift and other authors of his time, like Alexander Pope and Defoe, intuitively sensed that information and the language used to describe it create an impossible pattern of reversal and negation that can exist only in the imagination.[19] Taking this tendency to its extreme, the narrator of the *Tale* describes bodies turned inside out and men "whose intellectuals were overturned" (84, 77).[20] The narrator "ordered the carcass of a *beau* to be stripped in [his] presence" and "laid open his *brain*, his *heart*, and his *spleen*," only to find flaws on every surface (84). Religion and learning are "beautiful externals for the gratification of superficial readers," which the narrator sets out to "lay open by untwisting and unwinding" (31). As "laying open," reading is a visible process traceable by tearing away outer layers or by looking at the accessories of a coat. In each scenario, the inside and the outside are interchangeable and exchangeable.

From the narrator's perspective, the visible exteriorization of the reading process in the form of a collection leads to the complete internalization of a text's meanings without understanding them, giving readers confidence that they are the authors of the material contained within the collection. For example, in his dedication to John Lord Somers, the narrator notes that "being very unacquainted in the style and form of dedications," he hires some local wits to research past dedications and supply him with useful information to consult while he writes his own:

> In two days they brought me ten sheets of paper, filled up on every side. They swore to me that they had ransacked whatever could be found in the characters of Socrates, Aristides, Epaminondas, Cato, Tully, Atticus, and other hard names which I cannot now recollect. However, I have reason to believe they imposed upon my ignorance, because when I came to read over their collections, there was not a syllable there but what I and everybody else knew as well as themselves. (12)

The experience of reading the wits' notes on preface writing, which yields no new knowledge, at first seems a contrast to the hallucinatory effect of the elixir that makes its user see all the world's knowledge in the palm of his hand. Both encounters, however, actualize the dream of instant access; a vast quantity of information is reduced to a single text, the narrator is disoriented and loses his ability to "recollect" the names of the sources, and the information he ends up with is part of himself. The compilation, whether in elixir or note form, makes texts seem so accessible that readers become confident of their mastery of the ideas contained therein and experience literary déjà vu. Déjà vu is paramnesia, memory by feeling, a sudden illusion that a moment, thing, or idea is familiar, while the particulars of the meaning—the who, what, when, and where—are forgotten.[21] The narrator claims that something about collection recreates that kind of confidence in familiarity, convincing a reader through juxtaposition that he knows something he does not know.

The narrator finds the collected information about dedication writing familiar but cannot even recall some of the authors' names, just as the person taking the elixir cannot read the languages of the copies. Once excerpted in the wits' ten pages of notes, which is all the narrator has to consult, the originals cannot be re-collected. Collection, then, is a genre of erasure as much as it is a genre of accessibility. In order for universal access to remain a believable promise, texts and ideas must be sacrificed. The crowd at the beginning of the introduction may long for information that is "instantaneously accessible to the specialist and to the public," as Craven claims, but if only diluted, distilled, and excerpted versions of original texts are accessible, even specialists will have limited knowledge of their fields.

The narrator focuses on collections in part because their structures and affects on their readers reenact the unique issues at stake in an era coming to terms with information. On the one hand, information depends upon accessibility, a communicative ease exemplified by the simplified language of insides and outsides. One is either informed or not. To be accessible, in turn, the information must be made public. On the other hand, the presence of certain information necessarily means the absence of other information. A "series of decisions," in Lèvy's words, have been made by writer and readers that shape the text structurally and semantically (*Becoming* 55). Likewise, from the narrator's perspective, one crowd member's fantasy of "obtaining attention in public" by achieving a "certain degree of altitude" or "superior position of place" is another's nightmare of concealment (27). The elevation of one necessarily means the silencing of another, like texts excluded from collections and inevitably destroyed by Governor Time. Craven believes that the *Tale* surrenders to this inevitability and "engage[s] in the same frenetic competition to erect *the* superior mechanical information-delivery system above the heads of the crowd" (154). The result, he finds, is that "[c]ontent is subordinate to fixing the attention and sustaining an image" (154). Though the narrator does indicate that the space above the crowd is attractive in its emptiness, he does not go forward to elevate any individual image to draw the crowd's, or the reader's, attention. Metaphorically, he describes so many images and figures that it becomes impossible for the reader to "fix" her attention or "sustain an image" (154). The "virtual substitutes"—"a rainy day, a drunken vigil, a fit of the spleen, a course of the physic, a sleepy Sunday, an ill run at dice, a long tailor's bill"—distract rather than focus the reader's attention on a central image (*Discourse* 13, *Tale* 88). Thus, although the *Tale* is an attempt to find a better communication system, that system is neither mechanical nor "above the heads of the crowd" (154). Instead, the narrator abandons such vertically-dependent, hierarchical images of visibility in favor of ones that emphasize secrecy and the invisible. The individual who moves through the crowd without being seen is the one who best communicates with it.

By looking at the narrator's examination of "exposure" as it depends upon publicity yet encodes vulnerability and abandonment, readers can better understand how the *Tale* uses the tension between publicity and secrecy to revise assumptions about information. Like collections, exposure works through distraction. Exposure may indeed be the first step in reforming corrupt systems of learning, religion, and even information management, but the narrator questions whether exposure necessarily happens *only* through publicity. The problem with publicly exposing an institution or person in need of reform is that the public's attention is usually misdirected away from that institution or person and focused on the debate itself. To prove his point, he examines defamation, which he concludes is an ineffective attempt by writers and readers to enact change because it inevitably draws attention away from the issue. Rather than urging readers to abandon such practices, however, he learns how to profit from the diverting nature of defamation in order to develop a larger strategy of secrecy.

Defamation, the attempt to tell readers whom *not* to read or pay attention to, so often accomplishes the opposite.[22] The narrator muses that "whoever should mistake the nature of things so far as to drop but a single hint in public" about the flaws of others "must expect to be imprisoned for scandalum magnatum, to have challenges sent him, to be sued for defamation, and to be brought before the bar of the house" (24). The publicity of the insult, as well as the particularity of it, makes readers turn against the writer rather than question the reputation of the person defamed. In an image that resembles the crowd of the introduction, the narrator describes a "huge assembly" in which an overweight man "half stifled in the press" defames those responsible for assembling the gathering (21). He "cries out 'Lord! what a filthy crowd is here! Pray, good people, give way a little. Bless me! what a devil has raked this rabble together! Z__ds, what squeezing is this! Honest friend, remove your elbow" (21). A weaver standing nearby turns to insult him in turn, exclaiming, "Bring your own guts to a reasonable compass (and be d___n'd) and then I'll engage we shall have room enough for us all" (21). Defamation invites readers to participate in the issue, but the participation it inspires can be reactive rather than corrective.

As a publication that describes contemporary religious and education systems, the *Tale* turns defamation against itself, harnessing its tendency to distract readers from the real issues in order to create a religiously and politically charged text that operates subversively. By claiming to redirect the reader's attention away from Thomas Hobbes's *Leviathan* (1651) toward a tale of a tub, Swift redefines problems of religious and educational organization by professing to *not* look directly at them. The narrator complains that his critics "think it a more dangerous point to laugh at those corruptions in Religion, which they themselves must disapprove, than to endeavour pulling up those very foundations wherein all Christians have agreed," and so he adopts a counterstrategy of misdirection (3). Since critics would rather fight the satire than solve the problem, his strategy as secretary is to make satire the tub, to tempt readers to focus on the complicated figurative language and structural organization of the work as a means of diverting their attention elsewhere, to the real issue.[23] Pushing readers to exhaustion, the *Tale* lures its audience to avoid reading at all costs and at times goes so far as to *prohibit* its audience from reading. Yet at the same time, the narrator capitalizes on the inherent nature of defamation to challenge the targets of his satire—scientists, religious figures, politicians, and everyday reader alike—to retaliate in writing. In this way, the *Tale* invites a kind of hyper-participation in the text, reading that is also writing, authorship that is at once solitary and communal.

Though he repeatedly claims to "expose" corruption in religion and learning, the narrator recognizes near the end of the *Tale* that though he can make an issue visible, he cannot force the reader to stay focused on it or consider solutions. While in his apology of 1709 he wonders why "any clergyman of our church [would] be angry to see the follies of fanaticism and superstition exposed [. . .] since that is perhaps the most probable way to cure them," by the digression on madness he realizes that disclosure may be a better approach (2). Unlike exposure, which forces responsibility onto readers, disclosure figures readers as confidantes, as secretly informed partners with the opportunity to work collaboratively to reform the issue at hand. At first he seeks to "forc[e] into the light" and thus make vulnerable issues of reform, but finally he understands the value of "innuendoes" and secrets in using mystery and darkness to enact change (63, 90). In the digression on madness he admits that though "unmasking" and "the art of exposing weak sides" are similar practices, unmasking carries with it the connotation of "delusion," which holds readers' attention more effectively (83).

Using the metaphor of the knot, the narrator asks that readers become more self-conscious about the way in which important issues are discussed in public and private domains. In a knot, threads cross one another repeatedly in a mirror-like, intersecting pattern of reversal and progress as the knot becomes larger and more complex. A system built vertically or hierarchically can topple easily, but a system that is knot-like is almost impossible to disentangle, as Peter and Jack's struggles to tear embroidery from their coats proves. Francus concludes that Swift's reader "knows what kind of language to avoid, but there is no guidance as to what kind of rhetoric is appropriate to use" (103). Actually, the *Tale* offers a number of hints about appropriate language to use for conveying information, guiding readers and writers away from the linear images of surface and multi-layered depth and toward the tangled shapes of a knot or web, in which there are no insides or outsides, levels intersect, and parts shift and turn back upon themselves.

In his study of "LSDNA," information, and biotechnology, rhetorician Richard Doyle writes that "the undoing of one knot is the creation of another, not a bringing of secrets into the outside of knowledge, but the endless and unpredictable wander from knot to knot, problem to problem" (105). Doyle's description of the relationship between the knot and secrecy, and his challenge to the rhetoric of insides and outsides, is part of a larger project that confronts problems of replication in informational and biotechnological environments. In the terms the *Tale* offers, the replication of one text (or a piece of one text) for inclusion in a collection does not produce an exact copy of the original but an unpredictable new text because, like a strand of DNA, the copy carries with it a host of secrets, things not said or seen that are only apparent once the copy joins other copies to create a new work.

The narrator's metaphor of the knot works in the way Doyle describes, allowing parts of its structure to remain hidden from view until they are discovered by accident. When the footnote writer encounters a large typographical gap in the *Tale's* manuscript, he immediately begins referring to the work as a web: "Here is another defect in the manuscript; but I think the author did wisely, and that the matter which thus strained his faculties was not worth a solution; and it were well if all metaphysical cobweb problems were no otherwise answered" (82). The frequent defects in the manuscript, which occur most often when the narrator is about to "unravel" a "knotty point" of the *Tale,* tempt readers with information that is inaccessible to them. (82).[24] As soon as the narrator sets out to make a point "clear" the text is replaced by asterisks, which direct the reader's visual attention to the passage yet appear to hide the true meaning, tantalizing the reader with secrecy. Dustin Griffin believes that Swift, "though he plays with the conventional idea that the satirist seeks to 'reform' the world, seems concerned finally to 'vex' it: that is, to ruffle or disturb its smooth surfaces" (27).[25] Similarly, Mueller claims that the *Tale* "parodies modern bad writing" (206). Yet Swift's self-conscious experimentation with the rhetoric of information is an attempt to reform the metaphorical vocabulary his readers use when they speak and, more importantly, think about information. On a literal level, he actually does set out to replace language like "smooth surface" with terms like "ruffle," to push material assumptions about information as surface-level and vertically arranged toward words like "knot" and "cobweb" that can account for the importance of negation, reversal, and concealment in communication.

For the narrator, writing is a communicative process of discovery and collaboration best exemplified by analogies that capture the importance of wandering and pausing, of moving back and forth across a wide compass in a pattern that more resembles a ball of twine than a taxonomical chart:

> For in writing it is as in travelling: if a man is in haste to be at home [. . .] if his horse be tired with long riding and ill ways or be naturally a jade, I advise him clearly to make the straightest and the commonest road, be it ever so dirty. But then surely we must own such a man to be a scurvy companion at best; he spatters himself and his fellow-travellers at every step; all their thoughts, and wishes, and conversation, turn entirely upon the subject of their journey's end; and at every splash, and plunge, and stumble they heartily wish one another at the devil. (91–2)

If the traveler represents the writer, the horse in this passage stands for the reader. Concerns about the reader's stamina or impatience push the writer too quickly toward the point or conclusion of the text. Though initially the narrator seems to recommend that a writer satisfy the reader's needs, he enlarges the analogy in the next sentence to include the reader as a traveling partner, suggesting that writing and reading are collaborative ventures best enjoyed if both parties have the freedom to follow their fancy. A horse that walks slowly, is allowed to pause, and wanders off the path will not tire as fast as one driven to the final destination with great speed. Likewise, the traveler preoccupied with linearity frustrates the traveler who invites digression, spontaneous topics of discussion, and a free pace. In the last pages, the narrator characterizes his writing of the *Tale* in the same terms, concluding that "[a]fter so wide a compass as I have wandered, I do now gladly overtake and close in with my subject" (91).[26]

It is during the "Digression Concerning the Original, the Use, and Improvement of Madness in a Commonwealth" that the narrator brings together his observations on multiplicity as it has been approached textually, in collections, and linguistically, in the language of insides and outsides and publicity and secrecy, to reconsider the position of the individual pressed in the crowd. He characterizes madness as division and as a general condition of human nature: physically, bodies, individual or social, are split up into multiple parts and need someone "to solder and patch up the flaws" (84). Mentally, madness is a vapor within the body that attacks the brain, and socially it is a prince, a king, a philosopher, or even an author who terrorizes others seemingly without reason, competing with and conquering rather than conversing or collaborating with them (78–82). In these descriptions, madness is the unseen, an entity that works from a clandestine position within to reorganize the world around it. The secretary, like someone mad, is uniquely able to move inside and outside the community, speaking his own language of seeming unintelligibility as he attempts to hide and repair the threats that most citizens are not aware of. Such an individual must possess the curiosity necessary to pursue a subject wherever it digresses, though the consequences of such a curiosity are significant:

> In the proportion that credulity is a more peaceful possession of the mind than curiosity; so far preferable is that wisdom which converses about the surface, to that pretended philosophy which enters into the depth of things, and then comes grave back with the informations and discoveries that in the inside they are good for nothing. (83)

Using the term "information" for the first time in the *Tale,* the narrator admits that being uninformed and unsuspecting—being credulous—is saner than having access to "informations and discoveries" (83). In a sense, madness is the condition of information and secrecy. The mad citizen, the narrator tells us, has intelligence of matters that others do not.

The solution to the dilemma of the individual pressed by the crowd is to negotiate the madness: elevating oneself above the crowd, struggling toward a "superior position of place," and crying out "Lord! what a filthy crowd is here!" are unproductive (21). What is needed instead is a subtle underground secretarial network in which moving inside or outside are strategic, in which agents are able to cope with multiplicity by negotiating publicity and secrecy. Disagreeing with readers who have seen the *Tale* as "a demonstration of Swift's own madness," Michael De Porte claims that the digression on madness is productive, a working towards and not a breaking down (McMinn 20).[27] The digression, he writes, "seeks not only to explain madness, it also seeks to advise disturbed people on getting the most mileage out of their disorder and governments on turning mad citizens to the best account". (De Porte 174). De Porte does not speculate how exactly "mad citizens" may best serve their governments, but the *Tale* suggests that madness can be a new order (and not a "dis"order) of association, where the narrator's loss of control over the relationship between his reality and his virtual reality, between images he tries to describe and images he obsessively collects in order to make readers look at that thing differently, is a necessary step in the realization that one need not elevate himself to be heard in the crowd. In a world of textual surplus, clandestine approaches can be more effective. As a model of this type of movement, madness has a "use" in the commonwealth.

The narrator turns to secrecy as a strategy for communicating with his own reader; by pretending to "discover" (not uncover) a secret to the reader he is able to secure the reader's attention until the very last line of the *Tale* (103).[28] Michael F. Suarez agrees, concluding that the work invites readers "to a process of discovery—both in the ordinary meaning of the word and in its forensic sense of a sifting through the evidence provided by one's adversary" (115). Such a strategy, in the end, frees him from the crowd that squeezes the individual in the beginning of the work: "But now, since by the liberty and encouragement of the press, I am grown absolute master of the occasions and opportunities to expose the talents I have acquired, I already discover that the issues of my observanda begin to grow too large for the receipts" (103). Now liberated and "encouraged" by the press rather than stifled by it, the narrator is a "master" of a multiplicity that is infinite; like a knot, his collection of observations continues to grow in size and complexity (103). Fittingly, the final line of the *Tale*, where he decides to "here pause a while till I find, by feeling the world's pulse and my own, that it will be of absolute necessity (for us both) to resume my pen," is staged as a silence, and the narrator is so united with his audience that he is physically connected to them. If the world wants a sequel, the production will be collaborative: both writer and reader, "us" in the narrator's closing words, will take on the project together (103).

From the introduction to the final paragraph of the *Tale*, the opening image of the individual pressed by the crowd symbolizes the narrator's struggle to come to terms with the rhetoric of information that saturates his print culture, from the threat of overwhelming multiplicity to the promise of universal accessibility. That Swift addresses the question of whether collection and replication, as they make accessible yet erase the original text, are necessary steps in a society's negotiations with new information technologies goes against the timeline upon which media theorists have based their studies. The *Tale* thus suggests that such issues are not the unique concerns of a digital age, that media theory may indeed be confronting issues more fundamentally associated with human organizational tendencies than with technological consequence. Further, in his identification of the secretary as organizational genius and of the knot as metaphor for collectively constructed and structured texts, as well as his assessment of the confusing language of exteriority and interiority that characterized the contemporary vocabulary of his era's communication systems, Swift's narrator comes close to realizing the potential of print as a means of collaborative authorship, a possibility just beginning to be explored by thinkers like Lèvy, Hayles, and Epstein.[29]

Chapter Four

Infectious Information: Signs of Collective Intelligence in Defoe's *The Journal of the Plague Year*

One month after the bombings of the World Trade Centers on September 11, 2001, citizens across the United States received specific directions for the handling of mail suspected of contamination by anthrax.[1] One warning, circulated by electronic mail on a university campus, asks staff members to familiarize themselves with procedures on the following checklist:

> 1. Close the door to the office or section off the area to prevent others from entering. Move to an area that will minimize your exposure to others. Avoid contact with others when possible, and remain in the area. Wash your hands with soap and water to prevent spreading any powder to your face. Public Safety and Health responders will come to you.
>
> 2. Make a list of all people who were in the room/area or have since entered the area where the suspicious letter or parcel was recognized. (Crime 1)

On February 8, 1722, Daniel Defoe's *Due Preparations for the Plague, as well for Soul as Body* described a similar postal nightmare. In his portrayal of a model family that survives the plague because of efficient preparation, Defoe outlines an even more elaborate protocol than that illustrated in the university warning:

> His letters were brought by the postman, or letter carrier, to his porter, when he caused the porter to smoke them with brimstone and with gunpowder, then open them, and to sprinkle them with vinegar; then

he had them drawn up by the pulley, then smoked again with strong perfumes, and taking them with a pair of hair gloves, the hair outermost, he read them with a large reading glass which read at a great distance, and, as soon as they were read, burned them in the fire; and at last, the distemper raging more and more, he forbid his friends writing to him at all. (64)

Despite very different contexts, the twenty-first-century e-mail and the eighteenth-century publication on the plague record the vulnerability of information networks, like the postal system, under the threat of disaster. The documents, both warnings that depend upon quick circulation, must pass through the community like the infection they mean to deter; sent from one party to another, the survival of the message means the survival of its readership. The letters described in each message must also pass through the same channel that transmits the virus, so that any communication *about* infection could be communication *of* it.

Until contamination can be confirmed, recipients must isolate themselves and contain the suspected virus with virtual boundaries, transforming what was once ordinary office or domestic space into a visibly marked danger zone. The office worker, as directed, should "section off the area to prevent others from entering" (1). The man in Defoe's description shuts himself inside his home and takes extreme measures to put distance between himself and others. Even the letter itself is "read at a great distance" with a reading glass, and when the plague is at its height the man refuses to communicate with regular correspondents (*Due* 64). As Defoe's description highlights, the promise of distance communication—through an improved postal system and print publication—can become the burden of isolation in times of adversity. Expanded communication spaces can become sites of great danger. In information ages like the eighteenth and twenty-first centuries, mass media perpetuate collective trauma at the same time that they try to deter it.

"If global and instantaneous electronic witnessing opens new fields of action," Rodowick observes in a *PMLA* issue dedicated entirely to media states, "we miss their potential by calling up an Enlightenment concept of the public and a faith in the power of the image and the press to inform and in so doing to induce action" (22). Though speaking of technologies unique to the late twentieth and twenty-first centuries, Rodowick reiterates a common assumption about eighteenth-century attitudes toward their developing information systems when he states in passing that citizens of the period exhibited unwavering confidence in what they saw and read. As evidenced in *Due Preparations* and, even more convincingly, *A Journal of the Plague Year*,

Defoe, one of the most significant figures in the history of print journalism, certainly does not reflect a naïve "faith in the power of the image and the press to inform" (Rodowick 22). On the contrary, he demonstrates great concern for the dangers as well as the profits of the increased movement of people, goods, and ideas, as better transportation, more ambitious trade, and an expanded media state "open new fields of action" in the *Journal* (22). The *Journal* is preoccupied with the power of press and image as systems that potentially falsify, withhold, and misreport information. Specifically, H.F., the anonymous narrator and compulsive recorder and reporter of the *Journal*, details one eighteenth-century community's anxieties about misinformation in the midst of disaster, as suspected government secrecy perpetuates fear of systematic exclusion from the informed public sphere. At once dizzyingly expansive and claustrophobically constrictive, the media state of Defoe's plague-stricken London transforms disaster into news event.

For over ten years before the publication of the *Journal* in March of 1722, Defoe compulsively documented the 1665 plague, collecting contemporary correspondence and compiling it for publication, exhaustedly trying to prepare his fellow citizens for the virus's return. From October to December 1709, articles appeared in his *Review* warning of the probable spread of infection during the wars against the Second Coalition (Roberts viii). In August of 1712 he published an overview of outbreaks in Europe during the previous eight years, and later that same August he sent out a reminder of the London disaster by republishing the Mortality Bill of the week of September 12, 1665, by far the worst week of the epidemic when it was rumored that over 7,000 died within two hours (viii). From 1709 to 1722, Defoe published ten articles in *The Daily Post, Mist's Journal,* and *Applebee's Journal* arguing in favor of Walpole's Act of Quarantine, which would block commercial vessels suspected of carrying the disease (viii). Margaret Healy and Paula Backscheider read Defoe's plague writing as rhetoric to rally support for Walpole's Quarantine Act, and it may not be a coincidence that the Act was approved only four days after Defoe's publication of *Due Preparations. A Journal of the Plague Year* appeared just one month later. "Woven into the narrative," Backscheider writes, "the clauses of the Quarantine Act are worked out in H.F.'s observations" (*His Life* 489). In these writings, though particularly in the *Journal,* readers see Defoe working through the relationship between disaster and the media that describe it, between traumatic event and news of its occurrence.[2]

The *Journal,* constructed from personal reminiscences, parish records, official decrees, diagrams, medical records, bills, verse, oral and written myths passed down through generations, and even what appears to be an embedded travel narrative, exhibits the same obsessive documentation and publication of diverse information about disaster that is evident throughout Defoe's career. As Backscheider observes, the *Journal* seems to move "through documents": "The Lord Mayor's Order's alone comprise over one-thirtieth of the book" (*Ambition* 139). The anthrax warning in 2001, which asks citizens to "make a list of all people who were in the room" at the time of alleged exposure, functions much like Defoe's plague-writing—both emphasize the need for documentation of the event, so that the anthrax- or plague-contaminated letter becomes the impetus for other writings that, in turn, prompt even further documentation (1).[3] From its concern with the Bills of Mortality to its reflective consideration of itself as historical account, the *Journal* itself begins and ends with documents made public to inform citizens of the movement of the plague.

Looking back on the months preceding the outbreak, H.F. remembers the appearance of two comets that "pass'd directly over the City, and that so very near the Houses, that it was plain, they imported something peculiar to the City alone" (20). The comets follow similar but slightly different paths, marking the city as a potential danger zone and suggesting that the scale of human communication extends even to the stars, with the help of intergalactic message carriers. The sky itself communicates information that can be read and studied as closely as an individual's mail, as citizens interpret the first comet as sign of plague and the second as warning of the London fire. The double appearance, first of one comet and then another, also suggests the susceptibility of the atmosphere to multiple trespass through undetected, vulnerable open spaces. The comets bear down on the city from different, invisible points of entry and appear to carry with them secret messages about the city's future.

The astronomical bodies are at once distant and threateningly close as they "pass'd directly over the city" and yet are "at a distance, and but just perceivable" (20). Echoing the *Journal's* broader concern with the simultaneous expansion and restriction of the eighteenth-century media state, their appearance suggests that as communication networks expand with apparently infinite reach, geographical distance seems to decrease and the inevitable meetings between previously separated parties can be as potentially dangerous as they are profitable. Indeed, the comets illustrate the extreme of global communication with local delivery—passing so close to the houses, they seem to deliver their mysterious messages directly to citizens' doorsteps. Like many mass-delivered media, the comets allow only one-way communication, providing commentary on upcoming events inscribed in the sky like print on a page but denying citizens the opportunity to respond, to write back. Of course, comets were associated with prophecy long before Defoe's description. One of the first recorded comet sightings read as prophetic vision occurred in 87 BC during Julius Caesar's adolescence and, in hindsight, was reported to predict his later rule (Calder 25). The Norman Invasion of 1066 was also said to be signaled by a comet, which·is illustrated in the 1069 Bageaux Tapestry (25). What is striking about Defoe's depiction of the two comets is neither that his crowd reads them as prophetic nor that H.F. resists interpreting them as such, but that their spatial relation to the city echoes the *Journal's* larger concern with communication and the formation of a collective consciousness. Also interesting is H.F.'s explanation for his own skepticism: "natural Causes are assign'd by the Astronomers for such Things; and that their Motions, and even their Revolutions are calculated, or pretended to be calculated; so that they cannot be so perfectly call'd the Fore-runners, or the Fore-tellers, much less the procurers of such Events, as Pestilence, War, Fire, and the like" (20). Thanks to advancements like Haley's 1692 calculation, which accurately predicted a comet's return in 1758, the appearance of an astronomical body could be reported and documented before, and not only after, it occurred (Calder 25). Rather than wait for prophetic signs, humankind was finally capable of making its own predictions. The *Journal* itself, though not a prediction, certainly anticipates the 1720 plague as the return of the 1665 one. At this moment in the narrative, as H.F. diverts his focus away from the plague to discuss messages circulated before the event, he makes a prior occurrence part of his report, extending the narrative of the disaster back in time at the same time that he extends it forward to the distant future of the journal's composition.

Like his other writings on disaster, including *Due Preparations* and *The Storm* (1704), the *Journal* marks an historical point at which printed media actualize and prolong disaster, temporally forward and backward, as news event.[4] The list made by the twenty-first-century office worker could itself be contaminated, lost, inaccurate, or incomplete and, in due time, become the subject of news reports attempting to trace the moments directly following the exposure. In the same way, H.F. uncovers the inaccuracies and repercussions of the Bills of Mortality, which he finds do not represent accurate historical records of the spread of plague, but simply the spread of information about it.

News, such as the Mortality Bills or newspapers like the *Oxford Gazette*, attempt to represent the plague by framing it as a series of stories, controlling traumatic occurrences as news events as they classify, delete, and modify information. In the *Journal*, disaster reveals the limitations of human communication on both a local and global scale, highlighting the shortcomings of developing information technologies that indiscriminately circulate good news and bad news, accurate warning of the plague's approach and false notice of its dissipation. As feared by residents like the man who smokes his letters, new technologies can also deliver the danger itself. With the increased circulation of information comes increased circulation of harmful agents; messages move back and forth between parties and contaminants move back and forth between bodily tissues.[5] New communication spaces opened up by growing information systems like print and postal system become spaces in which unprecedented collective suffering can occur.

The *Journal* begins with H.F.'s consideration of the first circulated messages of the plague's approach, and he emphasizes the way in which citizens were initially informed of the virus and the great distance the virus probably traveled before reaching London. "It was about the Beginning of September 1664, that I, among the Rest of my Neighbours, heard in ordinary Discourse," he writes, "that the Plague was return'd again in Holland" (1). He continues: "it was brought, some said from Italy, others from the Levant among some Goods, which were brought home by their Turkey fleet; others said it was brought from *Candia,* others from *Cyprus*" (1). H.F. makes clear that news of the plague's approach reached various members of the community simultaneously and was not reserved for privileged individuals. Placing himself within a network of neighbors who communicate easily with one another on a person-to-person basis, H.F. exhibits relatively little interest in the origin of the plague when he concludes that "[i]t matter'd not, from whence it came; but all agreed, it was come into *Holland* again" (1). He implies that one distant location is the same as any other; all are part of a global information system that is intruding upon the town's comfortable communication spaces.[6]

H.F. defines his term, "ordinary Discourse," against old and new communication methods, explaining that messages about the plague "were gather'd from the Letters of Merchants, and others, who corresponded abroad, and from them was handed about by *Word of Mouth* only" (1). In 1665, H.F. depicts only merchants and some nameless others as "correspond[ing] abroad," and he stresses that verbal relay was the main means of transferring the message once within the city. Letters report global news, while local correspondence is limited.

As revealed by his descriptions of the months and days immediately preceding the plague's arrival, H.F. is as concerned with contemporary methods of correspondence as he is with the disease itself. Within his narrative of the 1665 plague is critical consideration of 1720 media, particularly the newspaper and official print publications. "We had no such things as printed News Papers," he informs his reader, "to spread Rumours and Reports of

Things; and to improve them by the Invention of Men, as I have liv'd to see practis'd since" (1). Print by no means protects London citizens from misinformation and distortion. H.F. then adds, though it is at first unclear whether he sees it as positive or negative, that "things did not spread instantly over the whole Nation, as they do now" (1). On one hand, instant information promises more advanced warnings of plague, which, unlike a storm or earthquake, moves more slowly and may be detected and thwarted. On the other hand, the dissemination of the plague is equated with the dissemination of infectious information as the reports "spread" to London, taking on the physical characteristics of pollutants (1).

Even more disturbing to H.F. than misinformation is the absence of information, and he becomes increasingly concerned with the distinction between the informed and the uninformed. Though citizens had to rely upon reports they received from discreditable sources, "the Government had a true Account of it" (1). Information becomes a source of power and authority as officials, in H.F.'s opinion, transform the plague into a grand secret to which only they are privy. "[A]11 was kept very private," he states, and as information about the plague's approach is withheld and "this Rumour died off again," London citizens "forget it, as a thing we were very little concern'd in" (1). Writing with hindsight, he implies that government secrecy is in large part to blame for the massive outbreak; when rumor is the first fatality of the disease, thousands are doomed to follow. Even though rumors may be inaccurate or distorted, they nonetheless keep citizens on the alert for danger. It is the piece of information that is missing, not the one that is exaggerated, that poses the real threat to H.F.'s community.

From September 1664 to March 1722, countless news reports, bills, and letters concerning the plague circulated in both H.F. and Defoe's communities. Despite this multiplicity of information, Defoe writes the *Journal* and depicts his narrator wandering the streets of London, searching for ways to understand the disease and its psychological impact on the city. With his seemingly immune narrator acting as a sort of on-site investigative reporter, Defoe compiles statistics, recounts personal stories, and creates a new narrative of 1665, adding one more document to scores of others and implying that a piece of information is indeed still missing from the puzzle that is plague.[7] Dori Laub focuses particularly on Holocaust survivors in his studies of traumatic narrative, but his observations also apply to the *Journal*. "In spite of the presence of ample documents," Laub writes, "he comes to look for something that is in fact nonexistent; a record that has yet to be made" (57). Continuing, he finds that "[m]assive trauma precludes its registration; the observing and recording mechanisms of the human mind are temporarily knocked out, malfunction" (57). Through fiction, Defoe places an observer in 1665 London who is somehow immune to the disease, who will not malfunction when he witnesses mass death, and who reports and documents every detail of the event to create a hyperreality of the plague. As he visits plague pits and infested ships in port, H.F. "testifies to an absence, to an event that has not yet come into existence, in spite of the overwhelming and compelling nature of the reality of its occurrence" (Laub 57). In his consideration of the Bills of Mortality, H.F. reveals that Laub's point is accurate but not complete in the context of the *Journal*, where plague may be impossible to register, but each of the many failed attempts to document it realizes the epidemic as news event. Readers may not experience the true "reality of its occurrence," but they do experience its *virtual* reality through print. As news event, the plague's status is repeated numerous times within short periods. For H.F., the effect is ironic: rather than better informing citizens and allowing them to do what they need to survive, the news provides what he calls "intermittent" information, "so they were as it were, allarm'd and unallarm'd again, and this several times, till it began to be familiar to them" (17). Citizens become "hardned" to information much like U.S. citizens after September 11, when the media reported numerous high-status terrorist alerts.

The *Journal* illustrates the extent to which, during times of disaster, citizens are affected by and rely upon written reports and updates to gauge their behavior. Though few react when, in December 1664, two physicians and a surgeon inspected the bodies of two London men, found evidence of plague, and "printed in the weekly Bill of Mortality in the usual manner, thus, Plague 2. Parishes infected 1," public response quickly falls in line with what is being printed (2). Hope fluctuates with the content of the materials that reach the community: "the next Week there seem'd to be some Hopes again," H.F. remembers, "the Bills were low, the Number of the Dead in all was but 388, there was none of the Plague" (5). In fact, the readers' responses become so aligned with the figures published that it becomes unclear whether the bills are reporting disaster or creating their own. Printed media actualize the event and create a narrative through numbers that readers can follow, experience, and act upon.

Several critics of the *Journal* have read H.F.'s commentary as supportive of news publications like the Bills of Mortality. For example, both Benjamin Moore and Manuel Schonhorn read H.F's use of the bills positively, as credentials for his credibility as narrator. Moore believes that the bills allow H.F. "to remove himself from the mass of rumors and anecdotes that make up most of the narrative and to reapproach the plague through supposedly authoritative quantification" (141). Schonhorn argues that H.F. "giv[es] life to fleshless statistics," in the process writing "a song of praise to an older England which could not have gone unnoticed by his eighteenth-century readers" (397). Similarly, Peter Earle observes, in his assessment of the bills, that plague "gave man far more notice than other illnesses of its visitation. Man could see it coming as its inexorable progress was charted by the newswriters" (279). Earle's point is part of a larger reading of the *Journal* that will also characterize Maximillian Novak's later interpretation that it "represents a concentration on the life of the poor such as never had been attempted before" ("Defoe" 221). From Earle's perspective the plague may kill indiscriminately, but its murderous impact is in part controlled by the media: the bills were "introduced to give the authorities an early warning of the onset of plague, a warning which, when published, enabled the rich to get out of town before it spread from the poor parishes to their own" (275).[8] Indeed, the bills may have had that original objective, but H.F. makes a point, in the first pages of the *Journal*, to portray ordinary citizens like himself, not wealthy Londoners, reading the bills. Regardless, Earle's point reveals that the bills occupy an authoritative position in the community discourse and that their printed statistics, whether accurate or not, influence public behavior.

Because plague is invisible, a faceless antagonist creeping through the city without witness, bills and other print media inevitably misrepresent it, classifying information in such a way that the plague takes on a misleading visual shape. For example, the summary "Collection of All the Bills of Mortality For this Present Year: Beginning the 27th of December 1664 and ending the 19th of December following" is divided into two main parts: the top half summarizes the total deaths in 1665 by geography, subdivided according to parish location, and the bottom records deaths according to apparent cause, listed in alphabetical order. Geographically, readers could see that parishes immediately outside the walls of London, in places like Middlesex and Surrey, were the most devastated, with St. Giles Cripplegate losing the most citizens: 4,838 residents out of 8,069 total deceased were lost to plague. Readers could also discover that while 625 women died in childbed, 21 were executed, and 46 died of grief, an overwhelming 68,596 were taken by plague. This reported statistic, 68,596, deterritorializes the plague and lifts it out of its original spatial and temporal frames, framing it in two new ways— by geographical impact and in relation to the other deaths of the year. Putting it another way, Scott J. Juengel finds that the bills are "too far removed from the accumulation of corpses that they purport to signify" (145). The bills urge a comparative analysis of the disease, temporally flattening it over the span of an entire year, depicting the illness as a singular event. And though the transmitted virus cannot be seen and moves indiscriminately among the general population, unconcerned about town limits, the bills separate parishes with clear boundaries according to their relation to London. The publication actualizes a rather tidy, consistent, and bounded event that in reality changes every hour, that moves without purpose or pattern, and that kills without regard for spatial or temporal frames.[9]

H.F. is frustrated with the way in which information is organized in the Bills of Mortality not only because it affects how citizens conduct themselves, but also because he recognizes that their statistics will form the basis of historical understanding of the plague. "Were the diseases and casualties of which people frequently die in this populous city rightly given into the bills of mortality," Defoe writes in *Due Preparations,* "many would be set down of other distempers than as we find them" (98). "Instead of hanged themselves (being distracted), and cut their own throats (being distracted)," he explains, "it would be said, hanged themselves (being in despair), and cut their own throats (being in dreadful trouble of mind); instead of pain in the head, it would be pain in the mind" (98). Defoe argues that the bills should distinguish between suicide because of insanity, temporary or chronic, and suicide because of depression or hopelessness. In the bill for the year 1665, no category exists for suicide victims. They could be listed under any number of categories, including "Distracted," "Drowned," "Found dead in streets, fields, etc.," "Grief," "Hang'd and made away themselves," "Murthered and Shot," or even "Overlaid and Starved" (1). In times of epidemic, such information could be extremely useful for public health officials trying to lessen the impact of disease during future mass exposures. Defoe's point is that events like the plague take many more lives than those actually recorded as plague in official documents, and that inevitably someone's death will be left out of the final plague count.

Defoe uses the example of suicide to support his argument that much information regarding the 1665 plague is missing not because it was unavailable at the time but because it did not fit into categories set by the government and media to report the event. Maurice Blanchot, however, sees data loss as inevitable in times of disaster, observing that it is "not simply as death at work that [plague] seems so singular a menace," but rather "its way of not letting itself be accounted for or brought to account, any more than suicide, which disappears from the statistics that are supposed to keep count of it" (87).[10] The virus defies accurate documentation because its scale and transmission are unprecedented and categories do not yet exist to record its behavior, but it also reveals conflicts already inherent in the society's communication systems. First, as Blanchot concludes in his consideration of cancer, plague "destroys the very idea of a program, blurring the exchange and the message" (86). A letter that describes the plague's effect in the sender's neighborhood, for example, even after it has been smoked with gunpowder and sprinkled with vinegar by Defoe's model householder, may pass on the virus. The mode of communication and the content of the message become confused. The program of which the letter's delivery is part is interrupted when the man burns the letter without writing back and, in the end, refuses to read or write any more letters at all. Postal systems with no mail break down.[11]

A letter sent to warn a citizen about the approaching plague that actually carries the disease itself and, once opened, infects the reader, seems at first to be the perfect example of McLuhan's confident statement that the medium, not the content of the message being delivered, has the real impact on what is communicated (7). Defoe, however, does not equate the medium of the letter with the warning it contains or argue for one's importance over another. Rather, he reveals anxiety that at the same time that something is said, written, read, and even interpreted, something unsaid and unwritten can be communicated without the listener or reader's knowledge. A secret message can be hidden within harmless everyday conversation when a single communication act is both expression and effect.[12] The consequences of the message—what will happen in the near future after it is heard or read—have actually already happened as soon as the message is delivered. Blanchot believes that fatal diseases like the plague and cancer "would seem to symbolize (and 'realize') the refusal to respond: here is a cell that doesn't hear the command" (86).[13] What Defoe suggests may be happening, however, is that the response occurs simultaneously with the question: "Do you have the plague?" is its own answer.

It could be argued that the secret message that communicates fatal disease, and not the disease itself, occupies the most menacing presence in the *Journal*. As he approaches September, H.F. discusses the impossibility of distinguishing between the healthy and the sick during the epidemic, stating that "it is impossible to know the infected People from the sound; or that the infected People should perfectly know themselves" (191). He continues:

It was very sad to reflect, how such a Person as this last mentioned above, had been a walking Destroyer, perhaps for a Week or Fortnight before that; how he had ruin'd those, that he would have hazarded his Life to save, and had been breathing Death upon them, even perhaps in his tender Kissing and Embracings of his own Children . . . if then the Blow is thus insensibly striking, if the Arrow flies thus unseen, and cannot be discovered; to what purpose are all the Schemes for shutting up or removing the sick People? (202)

Within familiar gestures of life and protection lie orders of death, commands that contradict the sender's intent. The only response to the unknown exposure, which could follow within hours or days, is the absolute absence of response—death.

Unable to decipher the hidden messages within plague-time discourse, H.F. and his neighbors become increasingly suspicious that important information they need to detect the virus is missing, and so he embarks on an investigative search for missing evidence. At one point he wonders if "it might be known by the smell of their Breath," but he quickly questions "who durst Smell to that Breath for his Information? Since to know it, he must draw the Stench of the Plague up into his own Brain, in order to distinguish the Smell!" (203). The plague, he realizes, confuses the exchange and the message (Blanchot 86). The airborne virus is actually transmitted at the very moment one citizen informs another that the plague is fast approaching, an unseen, unwelcome message that breaches the boundaries of the human body as it relays the breach of geographical ones. "Nothing could follow but Death," H.F. writes, "because it secretly, and unperceiv'd by others, or by themselves, communicated Death to those they convers'd with, the penetrating Poison insinuating itself into their Blood" (201).

H.F.'s fear of the plague as undisclosed secret quickly develops into anxiety that local communication spaces have become unfamiliar, foreign, and potentially life threatening. In his descriptions of various categories of "walking Destroyers," (202) for example, the saddler identifies the virus as foreign intruder and positions the victims in local spaces:

> These were the People that so often dropt down and fainted in the streets; for oftentimes they would go about the Streets to the last, till on a sudden they would sweat, grow faint, sit down at a Door and die: It is true, finding themselves thus, they would struggle hard to get Home to their own Doors, or at other Times would be just able to go in to their Houses and die instantly; other Times they would go about till they had the very Tokens come out upon them, and yet not know it, and would die in an Hour or two after they came Home, but be well as long as they were Abroad: *These* were the dangerous People, these were the People of whom the well People ought to have been afraid; but then *on the other side* it was impossible to know them. (191)

Interestingly, nearly every description in H.F.'s report involves a victim within close proximity to home. Anxieties about disappearing physical boundaries are offset by increased rhetorical focus on spaces like the home, local spaces with borders that are perceived to be more controllable. The juxtaposition of the body, vulnerable to trespass, and the home as familiar safe zone emphasizes one of the most difficult conflicts within H.F.'s media state. In contrast to the communication space of the human body, which offers multiple entrances, the home acts as metaphor of the single entryway in the beginning of the *Journal*.[14] The architecture of the victim's house allows a traceable and obvious path into and out of possible safety, while the body, as citizens were just discovering, is vulnerable to invasion by objects that cannot be perceived with the eye and that can enter and exit through immeasurable open spaces.[15] Under such conditions the human body, in its capability to transport simultaneous messages and things through multiple channels, becomes a place of infinite expansion.[16] Like the man who receives letters from friends abroad but must then shut himself off from the world when the plague becomes more infectious, the victim seeks out confined spaces in an attempt to counter the virus's expansive reach.[17]

At one point, H.F. is confined to his home and sits, in a seemingly safe seat, to witness the horrors outside, which are framed by his window. "Many dismal Spectacles represented themselves in my View," he writes, "out of my own Windows, and in our own Street, as that particularly from Harrow Alley, of the poor outrageous Creature which danced and sung in his Agony" (177).[18] Here, H.F. is separated from the disaster only by a sheet of glass, the event framed by the border of his window. Most shocking to him is the fact that the spectacle takes place in such close proximity to him, in the middle of familiar streets he has walked daily and in the center space of a window he still believes can keep out the infection.

The restriction of the man's suffering to the enclosed frame of the window is consistent with many other images in the *Journal* that confine spectacle to limited, highly defined visual spaces.[19] Before the official order to shut up houses, for example, H.F. walks through the city alongside many other residents, noticing that though "the Street was full of People, " everyone "walk'd in the middle of the Street, neither on one Side or other, because, as I suppose, they would not mingle with any Body that came out of Houses, or meet with Smells and Scents from Houses that might be infected" (17). Critics like John Warner argue that "[f]or H.F. the house stands as a safe retreat" if he "is willing to forswear involvement in history" and resist the urge to wander the city to report on the plague (46). However, H.F's early description of the street suggests his ambiguity about homes as safe zones when those homes are located in *urban* spaces. When he considers the row of houses on the London street, he is immediately struck with the number of entryways that open onto the sides of the road. Residents walk in the center of the street to put distance between themselves and the many doorways they pass, and their anxiety centers on entryways with open doors, not closed ones. The open door is thus transformed from a symbol of welcome into a symbol of trespass. Rather than encourage easy communication between local residents, the open door interrupts their correspondence.

During the height of the plague, neighbors avoid communication with one another in order to minimize their chances of infection. Once exposed to the virus, communication breaks down completely. Repeatedly in the *Journal*, characters lose the ability to communicate when the infection reaches its climax, and messages become scrambled once the virus has taken control of the body. For instance, after a mother discovers the "fatal Tokens" on her daughter's thighs, she immediately loses the ability to communicate with others (56). "Her Mother not being able to contain herself," H.F. recounts, "threw down her Candle, and shriekt out in such a frightful Manner, that it was enough to place Horror upon the stoutest Heart in the World." She then begins to run "up the Stairs and down the Stairs, like one distracted, and indeed really was distracted, and continued screeching and crying out for several Hours" (56). The mother is unable to respond to her daughter's situation with words, and the home, at first a safe zone, becomes a claustrophobic prison that perpetuates the mother's complete breakdown, which H.F. explains will be described generally as "distraction" in the Bills of Mortality (56).

The home as metaphor reveals a conflict within the local communication systems of H.F.'s London. In another striking story that H.F. recounts in his journal, for example, a man who has just learned that he has contracted the plague visits a family he knows well, just as they are sitting down to dinner:

> Another infected Person came, and knock'd at the Door of a Citizen's House, where they knew him very well; the Servant let him in, and being told the Master of the House was above, he ran up, and came into the Room to them as the whole Family was at supper: They began to rise up a little surpriz'd, not knowing what the Matter was, but he bid them sit still, he only came to take his leave of them. They ask'd him, Why Mr. ____ where are you going? Going, says he, I have got the Sickness, and shall die tomorrow Night. 'Tis easie to believe, though not to describe the Consternation they were all in, the Women and the Man's Daughters which were but little Girls, were frighted almost to Death, and got up, one running out at one Door, and one at another, some down-Stairs and some up-Stairs, and getting together as well as they could, lock'd themselves into their Chambers, and screamed out at the Window for Help. (160–61)

The home that would seem to offer a safe space for the family becomes a prison, and the visitor, once a friend, becomes a dangerous intruder. Rather than run out of the same front door through which the visitor entered, the family scatters to various corners of the home and yells out the windows as if they are trapped inside. The story emphasizes the single entryway of the house, through which the family cannot exit to escape his presence. The visitor leaves a contaminated path in the house that is symbolically singed into their memories, as they attempt to recover the use of their home by burning "a great variety of Fumes and Perfumes in all the Rooms" (161).

Most importantly, the family's physical avoidance of the man's path parallels the communication breakdown that occurs as soon as he informs them that he has contracted the disease. In Laub's terms, the visitor suffers from the "eighty-first blow"—having frantically sought out listeners to hear his story, he is denied his need to "keep alive the witnessing narration" (71). The family does not respond to the man's confession, shutting down all correspondence with him despite the fact that he is a longtime friend and neighbor, interrupting conversation just as it begins. After the man "went and open'd the Door, and went out and flung the Door after him," readers never see him again (161). H.F. acknowledges a gap in his memory, and he writes: "As to the poor Man whether he liv'd or dy'd I don't remember" (161). Even on a narrative level, then, information is missing. The door, flung closed, shuts out further information about the man's fate, and the narrative of the *Journal* quickly turns to other anecdotes, which offer multiple perspectives on the plague experience. The literal closure of the door is contradicted by the narrator's resistance to narrative closure. Novak interprets silences like these in H.F.'s narrative as reminiscent of a child's horror (*Master* 25). Recalling that Defoe experienced the plague as a child, Novak speculates that "the failure of language to describe the experience is very much the child's failure to find words to communicate his experience" (25). While this may be true, the inability of a witness like H.F. to describe a horrible event or provide closure to its narrative is more generally characteristic of the traumatic experience, regardless of the witness's age.

For H.F., anxiety about trespass and fear of the complete breakdown of London's communication systems are embodied by the figure of the night watchman. The watchman occupies a government-created position outside the homes of infected families, and his sole responsibility is to keep the family in communication with the community despite their complete containment. The watchman guards the entryways of the house in an attempt to maintain clear physical boundaries between the sick and the healthy.[20] H.F. recounts several stories of watchmen, during which he often focuses on the breakdown of communication between the guard and the family inside and on the final escape of the family through unwatched entries. For example, he tells the story of one watchman who hears a loud cry from inside the house but, upon knocking on the door, hears nothing. Finally, someone answers and asks him to stop the dead cart. The cart arrives and the men "call'd out several Times, *Bring out your Dead;* but no Body answered," H.F. writes, emphasizing the apparent refusal of the family to respond (49). In the end, the day and night watchmen inform the Lord Mayor, who orders a forced entry, and upon examining the house the watchmen learn that the family escaped through an undetected exit (48–50). H.F. notes that "it was impossible for one Man so to Guard all the Passages, as to prevent the escape of People, made desperate by the fright of their Circumstances" (52). In these accounts, H.F. tries to prove the ineffectiveness of the policy for shutting up houses, and in the process he draws a connection between physical and communication pathways that miss one another, emphasizing that interruptions in local correspondence may be symptomatic of larger problems. In this case, the family's lack of response reveals the secret of their escape, and potentially contaminated citizens now roam the city and pass the infection on to others.

Though the home offers unobserved entrances and exits, allowing parties to both intrude *upon* and escape *from* local spaces without detection, H.F.'s main concern is not with the impossibility of securing the local space but with the methods taken to keep distance between residents and trespassers, the healthy and the infected. The watchmen are compulsive witnesses, forced to observe the suffering of others from a close proximity while distancing themselves emotionally in order to perform their jobs.[21] Even though they stand so near the house, however, they inevitably miss the residents' escape because their position in relation to the house is so close. In other words, their perspective, apparently offering them more intimate observation, obstructs perception of the home on a larger scale. Information is missing from their view simply because they are focused too intently on the space before them. Similarly, the man who examines the letter with the reading glass may see the pores of the paper, but he misses the rat that scurries by in the distance, just outside his peripheral vision.

When they do not escape, Defoe's sequestered families, like the university staff members who are warned to section off their work areas, are separated from their communities and forced to wait out disaster in isolation. At the same time, the *Journal* records the isolation of the city at large from the rest of the world, its trade and communication cut off from correspondent nations. Indeed, H.F. is concerned not only with London citizens as individuals with private miseries, but also with the city's *collective* experience of catastrophe. For example, though the comets H.F. describes are distant from him in many of the same ways as the lone man who suffers outside his window, H.F. stresses his position as one within a large crowd that gathers to decipher the comets' messages. He even wonders why, after reading the comet as a sign of disaster, the people "did not rise as one Man, and abandon their Dwellings" (19).

Though his neighbors claim to read the comets as prophecy, to see phantoms, and to even hear voices, H.F. maintains that "they heard Voices that never spake, and saw Sights that never appear'd" (22). He concludes that the crowd's belief in signs is hallucinatory and hypochondriacal. In doing so, he identifies the development of a collective intelligence, a mass consciousness that evolves as a sort of coping mechanism for the disaster. The comet causes "almost universal melancholly" among his neighbors (20). A crowd looks for the figure of an angel in a cloud, and when one sees a face, another cries "What a glorious Creature he was!" (23). A man describes the motion of a graveyard ghost that walks toward him, moves away, and walks toward him again, until others in the crowd claim to see the ghost also (24). What H.F. describes is nothing less than the convergence of multiple individuals to build a single consciousness in response to the spectacle before them.[22] To deal with the overwhelming scale of the disaster, his neighbors collectively experience the sights before them and, as a result, build a temporary, alternative communication network that does not rely upon the type of person-to-person relay that could transmit the deadly virus.[23] They develop a sign system that relies upon group intelligence, in which information oscillates effortlessly between participants, without boundaries and without the marked entryways that are usually necessary in verbal or written relay, and in which any communication act is both expression and effect.

In their visions, the crowd sees phantoms that take human form, that occupy bodies and yet fill non-physical spaces. In his historical discussion of the human body, Lèvy claims that one step in the virtualization of the body is the emergence of a communal or shared body, which he calls a "hyperbody" (40). This hyperbody is able to conquer new spaces that can only be reached by "causing boundaries to tremble" (43). Bodies can enter and exit only through physical spaces like doorways; they cannot move through membranes or be carried away during inhalation. As an imagined collective, bodies once restricted become freely mobile. In this way, the group can take control of its environment.

The phantoms are also silent, and though the crowd calls out the figures never respond. Similarly, the graveyard ghost moves repeatedly toward a man and then retreats, indicating that though he has something to say he cannot speak. In their refusal or inability to respond to the crowd that longs for answers or at least acknowledgment of their questions, the phantoms H.F. describes represent the media state of plague-stricken London. Baudrillard sees media as part of an "institution of an irreversible model of communication without response" and wonders if the "absence of response can be understood as a counter strategy of the masses themselves in their encounter with power, and no longer at all as a strategy of power" (105). Print media, such as the bills, provide information for readers, but no channel exists for readers to send back their responses to that information; they can only receive information silently. Rather than see that silence as passivity, as a sign that the readers are controlled by the media or those in the business of gathering and reporting information, Baudrillard suggests the possibility that the readers use silence as a means of active participation in the media. In other words, they can stop reading a particular medium and seek an alternative means of learning about the event. In their attempts to adapt to the power of media during times of disaster, H.F.'s neighbors participate in a group event in which communication is unidirectional, an experience that counters their confrontations with potentially infectious verbal information and yet re-enacts the crisis of epidemic on a larger scale. The phantoms are like the plague virus: passing by a citizen's path, the virus is the medium and message of exchange yet it is unable to participate in that exchange as speaker. The virus withholds information of its presence, and the phantoms recreate that secrecy on the level of a temporarily visible human body.

Though his neighbors see angels in clouds and apocalypse in comets and H.F. "look'd as earnestly as the rest," he admits that he "could see nothing" (23). He stands outside the crowd, resistant to sharing its experience as if he fears being absorbed into the network. A reluctant participant who watches the crowd from the cool distance that characterizes all his chronicles in the *Journal*, H.F. challenges readers to ask, in Baudrillard's words: "is it the media that neutralizes meaning and that produces the 'unformed' (or informed) mass, or is it the mass that victoriously resists the media by diverting or absorbing all the messages which it produces without responding to them?" (105).

The *Journal* at first seems to be the product of one citizen's memory of 1665, but readers realize by the end that the work may also be the product of a collective effort. In other words, the *Journal*, as much fiction as fact, may mimic both the phantom and the virus in its narrative structure. The journal written by H.F. acts just as the crowd's vision does—it brings together multiple individual stories to form a total portrait of the plague as traumatic experience, drawing together distant parties within the same textual body, pointing to anecdotes and images as signs of larger lessons. A compilation of bills, diaries, and oral myths, the *Journal* certainly absorbs multiple messages about the plague, drawing readers' attention to the 1665 outbreak in order to warn them of the approaching Marseilles strain. And as a published book, the *Journal* passes through the community much like a virus. As Defoe states in *The Storm*, "Preaching of Sermons is speaking to a few of mankind. Printing of books is talking to the whole World" (1).

For Defoe, what is amazing about the disaster he reports in his compilation of personal stories in *The Storm* is that *all* of London and its surrounding rural environs felt the impact at the same time. The storm did not move slowly from one area to another but suddenly loosed itself upon the whole region, surprising residents of both city and country with simultaneous destruction. In this 1704 publication, Defoe gathers multiple narratives of personal suffering to construct a collective memory of the event. By the time of the *Journal,* Defoe takes disaster reportage one step closer to the kind of coverage to which twenty-first-century citizens are accustomed: he begins circulating reports of the plague *before* it arrives in London, *creating* a news event before it occurs. Yet while H.F.'s live coverage of the plague's approach may have been meant to prevent impending epidemic, his *Journal* is itself a communication space subject to the same secrets as the Bills of Mortality. As he looks out his window, H.F. may be able to witness a dying man without jeopardizing his immediate safety, but at the same time he inevitably misses events that take place far beyond the periphery of the pane. In this way, what Ian Chambers finds in his study of media and citizenship is ultimately applicable to the *Journal.* Defoe's work challenges readers to " invert the formula of considering the media as providing a window on the world and to think rather in terms of what the media are unable to see or hear" (26).

During most of the narrative, it seems as though H.F. is the only doorway through which readers enter and exit the London world of 1665. Just pages before the end of the work, however, before H.F. is finished narrating, readers receive a report of his death, as a parenthetical note, from an unknown editor. The editorial insertion occurs as H.F. describes a burial ground: "The author of this Journal lyes buried in that very Ground, but at his own Desire, his Sister having been buried there a few Years before" (233). Suddenly, the *Journal* is no longer the product of a single consciousness. This sudden interruption from the outside challenges the *Journal's* boundaries, revealing that H.F.'s private reflections are read by another before they are published, a faceless informer who may make other less visible changes. H.F.'s final words, "yet I alive!" lose their resonance since readers already know his fate; an editorial watchman keeps him from escaping the narrative alive. And like the suicide victims who are left out of the final plague count, the narrator's death escapes notice.[24] Though readers are not aware of it during most of the *Journal's* narrative, H.F.'s is a voice from the grave, a phantom referring to the unspeakable (Abraham 171).[25] Crucial to the collectively-intelligent group dynamic is that individual identities are temporarily erased, as the anonymous narrator's is when his death reveals that there may be multiple authors of the *Journal.* Even though isolation would seem to be the logical solution, the *Journal* demonstrates that citizens, both rich and poor, must realize that working together, as what one might today call a "hyper-body," will be more productive than segregating and confronting the virus individually.

Afterword

Toward a Material Poiesis of Information

There has emerged something "menacing," Walter Benjamin explains in his famous essay, "The Storyteller": "a form of communication which, no matter how far back its origin may lie, never before influenced the epic form in a decisive way. But now it does exert such an influence" (88). This "newer form of communication," he concludes dramatically, "is information" (88). It is clear, from the first pages of "The Storyteller" before he gives a name to this dangerous presence, that Benjamin equates information with death, just as Kittler and other theorists predict decades later in their studies of media and technology at the turn of the century. From Benjamin's perspective, information is one horrible sign that the world is in fast and furious decline. World wars, the Holocaust, the disappearance of storytelling and even of literature and the arts in general are the realities of an age in which information dominates human communication. When he claims that "never has experience been contradicted more thoroughly than strategic experience by tactical warfare, economic experience by inflation, bodily experience by mechanical warfare, moral experience by those in power," he means that warfare, inflation, and power politics are informational in nature and that information is somehow unnatural, inhumane, and threatening to the moral, economic, and even physical well-being of a culture (84).[1]

Recent discussions about information have rarely reached beyond Benjamin's prophecy that information is a menace. Still today, most studies of the concept are trapped between two extreme perspectives: either information is a great danger or it is the first step toward an enlightenment reminiscent of an idealized eighteenth-century quest for knowledge. For Benjamin, the more informed citizen experiences and understands less. For those in the business of mass media, the more informed citizen can make better choices. By arguing that eighteenth-century writers saw both the advantages and disadvantages of information and developed alternative management models, I am not attempting to rescue information from itself or from the inevitable extinction Benjamin describes. Rather, I seek to contribute a more complete historical picture than the usual binaries can provide.

Though they may not have been aware that they were participating in a discussion that would still be important three centuries later, Bunyan, Behn, Swift, and Defoe nonetheless capture community anxieties about the kind of menace Benjamin does not see emerging until World War I. Their works, however, do not merely reflect those anxieties; they challenge writers to experiment with new genres and narrative models, readers to adopt more careful interpretive strategies, and the community as a whole to recognize the ways in which secrecy, secretarial organization, publicity, and collective thought can help citizens cope with the threat, real or imagined, of information overload. Already portraying their communication systems in terms of journeys, highways, military strategy, suffocating crowds, knots, and viruses, these authors influenced the rhetoric of information as they critiqued the language already being used to describe it. Together, their writings begin to shape what Thurtle and Mitchell identify as a "material poiesis of information" (2). Thurtle and Mitchell's work seeks to "illuminate the ways that we perform the transformation from the virtual world of information to the actual world of flesh and bone," and the texts represented in *Fatal News*, I find, pursue a similar line of inquiry (2).

Keeping in mind that the term information is "inherently contextual," as Mitchell and Thurtle recognize it, readers meet Christiana, Isabella, Swift's anonymous narrator, and H.F. during moments of informational problem-solving (9). At the beginning of the second part of *Pilgrim's Progress* as she grieves for her husband, Christiana is confronted with two media—a post and a dream—that together cause her to rethink the structure and direction of her life. Isabella lives in a state of perpetual psychological torment throughout Behn's *History*, which religious and domestic vows, the postal system, and the local town news network only increase. She does not learn how to participate successfully in her communication system until it is too late. Swift's narrator seems to go mad by the end of his *Tale*, a psychological state that turns out to be more productive than Isabella's temporary insanity. For Swift, madness represents a necessary stage in the narrator's process of reorganizing information. Defoe's H.F., visibly torn between the providential and the empirical, narrates a reconstruction of the plague that proves more successful as a didactic tool than news reports, the Bills or Mortality, or even Defoe's more obvious argumentative social pieces, such as *Due Preparations for the Plague*.

Though his opinions are often extreme, Benjamin does offer a number of insights that can help to frame a conclusion about the eighteenth-century response to the idea of information overload. To explain how information is menacing, for example, Benjamin discusses the difference between global and local news, where global news constitutes the stuff of storytelling while local news, which he claims has become more popular because it can be "verified," is informational in nature (89). The main distinction between the global and the local, and thus between a story and information, is that the global cannot and should not be explained while the local, because facts can be checked, answers all of a reader or listener's questions. As readers can see most clearly in Behn's *History* and Defoe's *Journal,* anxieties about communication are often global in nature though they at first appear to be isolated local crises. Isabella's "fatal news" is delivered from a foreign source, and even her first husband's return is staged as the intrusion of a foreigner who needs "passport" to her home (219, 248). Similarly, Defoe's *Journal* begins with speculation about the plague as originating in another nation and traveling, through trade routes, to London. The plague is a threat from abroad. Even in *Pilgrim's Progress* the global potential of communication is taken to an extreme: citizens can communicate via post with the heavens.

Implicit in Benjamin's complaints is that information is an authoritative form of communication, that it explains too much about what it reports and consequently commands the reader or listener to interpret the meaning of an event in a certain way. Information is the one form of communication that cannot be interpreted because it has already been "shot through with explanation" (Benjamin 89). Bunyan, Behn, Swift, and Defoe all confront this same issue of informational authority; in fact, whether or not information has such authority, whether it merely "sounds plausible" but in reality is misleading, is a central concern in *Pilgrim's Progress,* the *History,* the *Tale,* and the *Journal.* As Maja-Lisa von Sneidern notes in an analysis of Swift, there was no way for early eighteenth-century readers to "measure" or "authenticate" sources, "no way to staunch the flood of words" (15). The titles alone of Behn, Swift, and Defoe's works emphasize each author's experimentation with the fine line between fiction and fact, information and misinformation. Participating in a contemporary title trend, Behn's novel, for example, is introduced as a true history. The narrator remarks that Isabella's biography is on record in her hometown of Iper yet, at the same time, makes grand claims that the "whole world" knows Isabella's story (257).[2] Preventing the reader from verifying global information, the narrator purposely refuses to discuss the war abroad, staying with the local story of Isabella's demise. In the *History,* then, information, the story, and the novel are not at odds with one another but in dialogue. Calling his work a "Tale" is obviously tongue-in-cheek for Swift, whose narrator makes it impossible for readers to decide whether Swift is mocking the form or lamenting its disappearance in the age of commonplace books and collections. Mueller notes Swift's concern with authority, though she focuses on contemporary perceptions of print and the book. She believes that, in the end, the *Tale* "parodies the bad writing he fears," bad writing that is a direct result of the perceived authority of print (208). As I have attempted to prove, the *Tale* is not simply an imitation. Similarly, one of Defoe's main concerns in the *Journal* is whether or not the Bills of Mortality and similar public reports should have authority in the community discourse. That he chooses to call his work a "journal" is perhaps a strategy for avoiding such suspicion of misinformation.

Seventeenth- and eighteenth-century authors wrote not out of naïve passivity and surrender to the threat of information but as aware and active participants in a conversation about how citizens might more efficiently manage information. That in the process of describing alternative systems they created texts that still today challenge generic boundaries may not be coincidental. The relationship between the emerging concept of information and the development of new genres, like the novel, has been unexplored. Behn's *History*, for example, oscillates between the novel and the romance in critical treatments. Ian Watt's critical terms would position the *History* with the romance, while more recent scholars like Josephine Donovan and Deborah Ross reclaim women authors such as Behn as novelists. Defoe's *Journal*, sometimes identified as an early novel, nevertheless differs significantly both from his other novels, like *Robinson Crusoe* (1719) and *Roxana* (1724), and from political and social writings such as *Due Preparations*. Hammond points out that the *Tale* may well be Swift's parody of the novel (85). In various ways, these works experiment with literary form by challenging generic boundaries even before those boundaries are clear.[3]

That works by Bunyan, Behn, Swift, and Defoe test definitions of the novel—all have been puzzled over as a possible "first" or early novels, for instance—suggests that what makes a novel has something to do with how that work approaches information. The novel develops at the same time that authors experimenting with it are defining what information is. Walter Reed argues that one defining characteristic of the novel is that it is inherently self-reflexive and continuously questioning its generic status. Similarly, information is always tested against itself in terms of whether a given piece of information is actually informative or not. Christian and Christiana are challenged, at each obstacle on the path to the Celestial City, to believe the unbelievable and verify their behavior using Scripture. *Pilgrim's Progress* teaches readers that just because certain information may not seem plausible—plausibility is one of the defining characteristics of information for Benjamin—a reader must still keep faith in its truth. For example, Christian's discovery that his city will be destroyed is unbelievable to his family and neighbors, and Christiana's neighbors at first doubt her letter from God. Reading their journeys within the context of information rather than solely as demonstrations of the process of Puritan salvation, it becomes apparent that the unique format of the work—scholars today still debate whether or not it is an allegory—reflects its commentary on faith as an informational as well as spiritual challenge.

In the case of Behn's *History,* readers encounter a novel in disguise as information, as a mere report of local news. As Benjamin would perhaps notice, the narrator even attempts to explain the moral for the reader. Yet the narrator's matter-of-fact interpretation, that the reader should learn the consequences of breaking vows, might well be sarcasm. Like Benjamin's storyteller, then, Behn's narrator leaves a great deal of room for the reader to form her own psychological response to the narrative. Throughout the narrative itself, readers are led to question how much authority letters, gossip, and town discourse in general should hold. In Swift's *Tale,* the narrator's view of information constantly turns back upon itself until the narrative is as complicated as the knots that hold the brothers' coats together. By advertising itself as a personal and potentially biased narrative—by denouncing its authority as "fact"—Defoe's *Journal* achieves the plausibility that Benjamin grants information. Yet while his goal seems to be to provide readers with as much information as possible about what happens to communities during epidemic, H.F. refuses to interpret the plague for his readers.

Ironically, the history of the *Journal's* critical reception reflects this same concern with informational authority. From the beginning, critics of the *Journal* focused on the work's status as a document, mimicking Defoe in their attempts to ascertain the accuracy or inaccuracy of the work as historical record of the plague. Throughout the eighteenth and nineteenth centuries, the *Journal* was regarded as historically authentic in its portrayal of the plague of 1665, and the *Journal's* influence can be seen in most of the plague writings that followed. Harrison Ainsworth's *Old St. Pauls: A Tale of the Plague and the Fire* (1841), the first nineteenth-century adaptation, is a long fictional portrayal of particular characters from Defoe's work as if they were historical figures, expanding on their experiences. In 1924, Walter George Bell published his version, *The Great Plague in London in 1665.* Bell was appalled that anyone could have considered the *Journal* factual and vowed to set the record straight by writing his historiography of the 1665 outbreak. Even in their critical histories, then, these four texts have inspired debate about genre, and those conversations have pivoted upon each author's critique of information.

Building from McLuhan's claim that media like print force citizens to adopt new "habits of perception," each of these works is also concerned with *routines* of communication on the collective level, specifically in terms of reading (23). A reading of the second part of *Pilgrim's Progress* in terms of information and communication, for instance, reveals a more specific consideration of how replicability and more open and numerous routes of communication necessitate new practices for reading texts the second time. The second part teaches readers that the interpretative process does not end once an initial understanding of the text has been reached, that not only should readers continue to reread the same texts with an attitude open to new meaning but that the text itself is dynamic and always in a state of semantic metamorphosis. To use a simple example, the second part asks readers to consider how they would read the Christian journey differently with and without the threat of an obstacle like the Giant Despair. While Bunyan warns readers of the dangers of habitual reading, Swift points to the increasingly unclear distinction between reading and writing since the appearance and popularity of genres like commonplace books and collections. The *Tale* focuses primarily on collections, as compilations of previously published works and as cooperative authorial productions, and argues that in their exteriorization of their textual histories collections conflate the acts of reading and writing. Defoe's *Journal* is as much a collective portrait of its contemporary media state as it is a history of one citizen's personal experience.

Each author begins with communities that fail to organize themselves or think together in order to confront threat; in the case of *Pilgrim's Progress* and the *Journal,* the threat is impending fatal catastrophe. Yet by the end of these narratives, communities have learned how to communicate more effectively using secret strategies. In *Pilgrim's Progress,* for example, Christian's community is uninterested in secret information, yet in Christiana's part the community operates on the assumption that secrecy is the most effective way to pass on information to others. In Behn's *History,* readers witness the emergence of information as both a public and a private activity, as not simply something citizens read or have access to but as something they *do* or *participate in* even if that means operating covertly. Defoe's *Journal* shows that print genres like the Bills of Mortality may strive for "universal access," but it is unclear what they offer access *to.* In his *Tale,* Swift recognizes the emergence of secretarial, or organizational, genius as part of his era's increasing obsession with collecting and collections. Secretaries perform the dual role of administering secrecy and of managing government and civilian correspondence. That such a position gains bureaucratic importance in the mid-seventeenth century and continues to develop as a significant office through the eighteenth century suggests that

Habermas's claims about publicity are helpful as general statements but difficult to apply practically in specific historical contexts. In addition, the narrator
of Swift's *Tale* confronts the issue of universal access directly, presenting a text
that is collectively constructed *by* its readers. By the end of the *Tale*, the public
has *become* the text to which it seeks access. Like *Pilgrim's Progress*, the *Tale*
questions whether publicity is the most effective way to communicate in a
modern media state, assessing the importance of secrecy during the later eighteenth century. Both writings also trace the consequences of the era's expanding bureaucratization of information at the administrative level. Secrets need
groups to survive. In this way, passed simultaneously on from one individual to
another, secrecy is a demonstration of collective action.

In his influential study, Habermas claims that by the end of the eighteenth century the public sphere, a communicative space between individuals
and the state in which rational decisions can be made, became instead a place
of exploitation, monopoly, and mass control rather than a space for group
cooperation.[4] Terranova agrees with Habermas's analysis, writing that "media
power, specifically the power of the mass media, appears as partially incompatible with the eighteenth century's model of political communication" (133).
Analyzing Bunyan, Behn, Swift, and Defoe's writings, however, one finds that
Habermas's assumptions about publicity and universal access simplify the crucial role that secrecy plays between 1678 and 1724 and, in turn, that underes-
timation of secrecy may misdirect Habermas in his final assessment of the
public sphere. In these works, secrecy and the power of the secretive encour-
ages a type of collaborative group action that inspires what we would today call
collective intelligence rather than mindless mass influence.

Michael Wutz urges that "[m]edia theorists must take note of the relationship between technological systems and what—to provide a sampling of the
most widely deployed adjectives—has been called collective, communicative,
cultural, connective, interactive, transactive, or social memory" (7). Terranova
summarizes that the "question of media and communications has thus been
related mainly to the problem of how a hegemonic consensus emerges out of
the articulation of diverse interests" (8). Wutz's redefinition of the relationship
in terms of shared memory is part of a larger trend in media studies toward considerations of collective intelligence. Though media theorists have not considered the possibility of collective intelligence, or of conversations about it, before
the twentieth century, Swift's and Defoe's works anticipate a future in which
information technologies, specifically print, will create a public organized and
collaborative enough to think as one entity. Swift, like Defoe after him in the
Journal, finds in contemporary communication systems the possibility of collective intelligence even though Swift was less enthusiastic than Defoe about this

prospect. While Swift revises the rhetoric of information in terms of webs, knots, and networks to imagine a collectively intelligent though dubiously reasonable public that communicates through collaborative rather than competitive genres, Defoe sees the London community's use of supernatural signs, like phantoms, as coping mechanisms that allow citizens to act as their own decentralized media. And as Bunyan scholars have pointed out, the second part of *Pilgrim's Progress* is about the community that forms around and collaborates with Christiana, which is in start contrast to Christian's isolation in the first part. For those, such as Hannah Barker, who doubt the usefulness of Habermas's concept of the public sphere, collective intelligence may offer a more fruitful way of thinking about the organization of the eighteenth-century public, at least as imagined by authors like Bunyan, Behn, Swift, and Defoe.[5]

All four works, as they seek a more sophisticated language with which to discuss information and communication, raise more specific questions about the collectively intelligent potential of religion. It is not coincidental that the bulk of scholarly work on all four of these works, in fact, is concerned with each author's concerns about religious reform and personal spirituality. Carol Flynn, for example, finds that "H.F. stands as a man of religious faith crossing warily over into the age of enlightenment, a man who consults his bible to plan his course but demonstrates at the same time that providential patterns cannot quite hold the plague in place" (8). Similarly, John Richetti observes that H.F. "speaks for the new secular age of triumphant British commerce and imperialism, [. . .]but he is also tied to that Christian world of sin and guilt" (32). Implied in both Flynn and Richetti's studies, and in studies of Bunyan, Behn, and Swift as well, is a hypothesis of fundamental importance in theoretical studies of communication: that modern and technological understandings of experience potentially displace spiritual understandings. It is the threat of this displacement that, in the end, may most worry Benjamin. Though he at first seems only to be grieving the death of storytelling, his description of an individual standing alone in the country, gazing toward the heavens, more resembles a lament for the lost spirituality of the Information Age citizen:

> A generation that had gone to school on a horse-drawn streetcar now stood under the open sky in a countryside in which nothing remained unchanged but the clouds, and beneath these clouds, in a field of force of destructive torrents and explosions, was the tiny, fragile human body. (84)

The world of information, in this description with its "destructive torrents and explosions," is unnatural. Its dominance, as a form of communication, means extermination rather than evolutionary extinction. The only protection the vulnerable human body can seek is spiritual, in the space represented by the clouds, yet the figure in Benjamin's imagination is too overwhelmed by the speed and multiplicity of his environment to appreciate it.

Throughout the late seventeenth and eighteenth centuries, communication systems transformed the religious landscape. Heise finds that twentieth- and twenty-first-century media theorists have acknowledged *cultural* transformations, but she does not mention any religious effects.[6] This connection deserves further analysis and may well be the next logical step for eighteenth-century scholars interested in media studies. Readers should remember, for example, that in the second part of *Pilgrim's Progress* Christiana and other citizens of the City of Destruction take their town's communication systems for granted until they are in contact with the Celestial City. It is only when she receives a post from God that Christiana realizes she is also part of another communication system. Newly conscious of the connection between herself and others, she is able to take decisive steps toward a reunion with her husband. God's post highlights the potential of postal communication for facilitating individual and community religious reform. Further, the narrator recognizes the relationship between various communication systems, particularly the post and print, and the social behavior of the allegorical characters about whom he dreams. *Pilgrim's Progress,* like the *History,* the *Tale,* and the *Journal* after it, portrays a system of religion rooted in cooperative citizenship made possible by multiple media.

It is not coincidental that the final chapter ends with Baudrillard, who focuses on the power of crowds that are not consciously rational but that, as Lèvy goes on to explain more clearly and hopefully, are capable of collective intelligence. Decentralized media disperse and fragment bodies that unite at unpredictable moments to create the virtual—alternative solutions for the unprecedented and overwhelming. Defoe's crowd gazes at a phantom it imagines as a collective body in order to deal with the overwhelming personal and community loss by plague. The union of these citizens brings readers back to the divine vision and revelation that is so important in Christian and Christiana's communities. Defoe's phantom, discussed by the crowd, as well as Christiana's letter from God and private vision of Secret, as they are shared by a community by the end of her ordeal, prove that oral and print media are both crucial in the emergence of a collectively intelligent body. Like *Pilgrim's Progress,* the *Journal* traces a process of problem solving, however successful or unsuccessful, and it is problem solving that defines the virtual. Virtuality is openness to the improbable and the inventive. It is Christian defeating Apollyon and Christiana, as a woman, completing her journey. It is Henault opening his eyes after death and Defoe's phantom hovering above H.F.'s neighbors. When H.F. stands outside the crowd, readers must imagine whether they would themselves be an H.F. or a member of the crowd. By forcing readers to ask themselves, "What would I do in that situation?" Defoe and his contemporaries encourage readers to consider their own responses to the threat of overload, to choose their alternatives and, in the end, to fashion their own virtual realities.

Notes

NOTES TO THE INTRODUCTION

1. By production, however, I do not mean to invoke a common link, in information studies, between information and industrialism. See Ian Miles's "The New Post-Industrial State" for a correlation of these terms.

2. Terranova admits, however, that "communication has never only been about the sunshine of reason illuminating the dark secrets of governance, but it has always cast its own shadows—those of a manipulation that takes as its object blind passions of the masses" (133).

3. Bristol and Marotti believe that McLuhan's central claim, that sense ratios change in response to new media, "is not a particularly controversial argument" (2).

4. Duff once mentions Bolter, a humanist scholar, but he does so only to acknowledge that Bolter's studies have become popular amongst "the arts and humanities intelligentsia" (163).

5. Admittedly, such views are more common in mid-twentieth-century media studies and in analyses conducted by those who quarry media theory for specific facts but are not familiar with the larger discipline.

6. May notes the problems with claims that major technological innovation is necessarily "revolutionary" and summarizes how parallels are often drawn between printing, industrialism, and the computer as technological impetus for a new "age" of some sort (13). Certainly such developments affected economies, communities, and even psychologies, yet too often the focus on machines like the printing press and the computer have obscured important developments in human organizational tendencies.

7. Rabb claims that "since the advent of print culture in the seventeenth century (and its later variation in the nineteenth-century printing of film), no intervening revolution in communication has occurred of the magnitude of the recent advent of the world wide web" (350). Standage, who sees the telegraph as an

even more revolutionary technology than either print or the Internet because of its unprecedented and seemingly overnight global reach, would certainly disagree.

8. Duff is most concerned with the methodology behind each of these conceptions of information and about whether they are valid ways of thinking of twenty-first-century information societies. He critiques the ways in which information is often discussed in academic and popular literature, remarking that generally treatment of information has lacked scholarly rigor and relies upon clichés and untested assumptions.

9. Capurro claims that the word "information" was used as early as the fourteenth century to mean the "moulding of the mind or character, training, instruction, teaching" but was later replaced by *angelia,* or "message" (262). The displacement, Capurro continues, "is indeed a clear sign of change, i.e. of the emergence of new and different kinds of institutions and practices concerned with the process of transmitting knowledge, of teaching and learning" (262). Then, during the Middle Ages, information is more specifically the "'good message' supposed to bring forth truth and salvation" (263). He concludes that this focus on message transforms *logos* into a *sacra doctrina,* which became increasingly important in the Roman Catholic Church, the universities, and other institutions.

10. Eisenstein does admit, after all, that "[a]mong historians dealing with the post-Reformation era, the invisibility of the *cumulative* impact exerted by the new communications system is particularly marked" (29 my emphasis).

11. Though her acknowledgement that studies of communication should take into consideration the cumulative as well as specific influences of particular technologies is an important contribution to media studies, Hesse's assumptions about the eighteenth century render an incomplete and even misleading image of the era's literary culture. In her quarrel with the idea of the "printing press as the great agent of Enlightenment and human progress," she convincingly impeaches machinery, but by considering the century as the "Enlightenment," she reveals her reliance upon stereotypes of the century to reach her conclusions (23). Twentieth- and twenty-first-century references to the century as an "Enlightenment," a term increasingly used with pejorative inflections, often imply that the century's citizens exercised naïve over-confidence in technological and scientific progress.

12. Terranova imagines information as "threatening us with the final annihilation of space-time and the materiality of embodiment" (2).

13. Marvin calls this kind of language "propaganda" (61).

14. Duff believes that the field of information theory "has robbed 'information' of its semantic content" by defining the term as merely a loss or gain of meaning (27).

15. As Brown notes, this "image of the breeding, multiplying text extends beyond scripture to all spiritually efficacious books" at the end of the seventeenth century (28).

NOTES TO CHAPTER ONE

1. Lynch believes that because Bunyan wrote other works between the first and second parts, including *The Life and Death of Mr. Badman* (1680) and *The Holy War* (1682), linking parts one and two sacrifices "creative continuity" (154). "Perhaps it is simply impossible to situate this work," Lynch concludes (154).

2. It is important to point out that I am not arguing that the Celestial City, as it represents a mass society in the imaginations of those who seek it, is *created by* changes in reading and interpretation habits, by developing communication systems, by new information technologies, or by modified systems of inheritance. Rather, I want to stress that the Celestial City and the diverse members of its community are *revealed by* the communication system in which the Man participates when he suddenly recognizes an apocalyptic message in scripture and joins an expansive network of citizens joined only by the fact that they all *made it* there. Connections never seen before emerge in the narrator's vision; a new sense of association, independent of geography, ethnicity, class, or nation, binds Christian, his family, and our narrator to an imagined community located far from the native land.

3. As Hancock finds, "Bunyan positions women on the boundary between a culture dominated by oral communication and one shaped by literacy" (76–7).

4. Of course, it is the narrator of *Pilgrim's Progress* who initially refers to the Bible as "a Book" and not as scripture, but Christian uses the same wording in his dialogue (8).

5. According to Newey, *Pilgrim's Progress* highlights not only the Puritan emphasis on the internal mental and spiritual life of the individual, but also "the individual's constant involvement in acts of interpretation and decipherment" (189–90). Fish goes so far as to conclude that "issues in *Pilgrim's Progress* are always interpretative" (238).

6. Swaim would possibly disagree here, since she feels that Christiana reaches the Celestial City because Christian provides her with "credentials" and Great-Heart facilitates her entrance to House Beautiful (158). I am not arguing that Christiana is fully responsible for her relatively easy and successful journey, however, but that Christian's "credentials" are public knowledge simply because they have been recorded. Great-Heart's assistance on the journey after House Beautiful is actually secured via post, when Christiana mails the Interpreter to request that Great-Heart be allowed to accompany her family further on the journey.

7. Robinson's study is one of the most comprehensive and thoroughly researched histories of the British postal service. Few studies of postal systems before the Industrial Revolution are available, and most that exist were published during the early decades of the twentieth century, such as J.C. Hemmeon's *The History of the British Post Office* (1912), Sir Evelyn Murray's *The Post Office* (1927), and Kenneth Ellis's *The Post Office in the Eighteenth Century* (1958). More recent histories include Tony Gammons's *The Early Days of the Postal Service* (1986) and Christopher Browne's *Getting the Message: The Story of the British Post Office* (1993), which borrows large sections from Robinson's work without attribution. Twenty-first-century studies discuss the postal system only in comparison with electronic mail delivery.

8. Swaim does not consider the role of mail correspondence in *Pilgrim's Progress* or draw a connection between spiritual and postal delivery, but she does reach a similar conclusion about Christiana's reception of the invitation to the Celestial City when she finds that "distinctions between Christians who inherit the promises through faith (like Christian) and those who inherit through patience (like Christiana) governs the death scenes as well as the departures" (182).

9. Keeble asks why Christiana goes on pilgrimage and speculates that Bunyan's answer would be her "natural affection for her husband, self-recrimination at her treatment of him and the encouragement of his example" (10). What Keeble overlooks, however, is Sagacity's description of her psychology before she takes her children through the gate. Certainly self-recriminating, Christiana seems on the edge of suicide, not salvation; she apologizes to their children for driving their father away and laments that it is too late to join him (Bunyan 146). At the height of her depression and hopelessness, Christiana is then delivered the biography of her sins, which, coupled with the letter from God, persuades her to go on the pilgrimage.

10. What is more interesting to Breen is that Christiana's ability to read seems to, in Bunyan's eyes, challenge his ability as an author to write the truth: "*The Pilgrim's Progress* equation of female literacy with authorial disempowerment proves a vexing inheritance for novels committed to recounting female *Bildung*" (98).

11. The precedent for Timorous's assumption that Christiana is insane appears in scripture, of course; for example, in Corinthians Paul the Apostle writes that "If therefore the whole church be come together into one place, and all speak with tongues, and there come in those that are unlearned, or unbelievers, will they not say that ye are mad?" (1:14:23). Christian's family and neighbors also thought he was insane after he read of apocalypse in his book, but their misunderstanding is not described as it is here in Christiana's section. When Christian returns home, distraught by his discovery, his family understands what he says but simply does not believe him, assuming that a "frenzy distemper had got into his head" (8). The next morning he attempts to speak with

them again, but the narrator states that they "began to be hardened" (8). It is at this point, then, that Christian and his family cease to communicate with one another. The breakdown of understanding between Christiana and her neighbors is more sudden and noticeable. Listeners may disbelieve Christian's message, but they do not doubt that he intends his meaning to be taken literally. Christiana's neighbors, however, at first think that Christiana speaks metaphorically, that she is actually telling them that she is about to murder her children and commit suicide.

12. Sadler makes a similar point about the use of literal language in the second part, noting that "[e]uphemism and indirection to some degree obstructed the fact of death in Part I of *Pilgrim's Progress;* but in part II, Christiana talks to her sons about the *death* of their father" (100). Graham would interpret the scene differently and focus on the fact that Bunyan usually characterizes "ungodly language," or the language of the neighbors, as feminine (20). Graham's main claim is that *Pilgrim's Progress* demonstrates, in the end, that both men and women are capable of this feminized ungodly language.

13. Questions surrounding allegory reiterate the conflict of the neighbor women's dialogue. While some critics look to definitions of allegory as the literary form of unmanageable multiplicity, of copious signification, others, such as Cope, conclude that in "the enclosure-obsessed eighteenth century, the collapsing space of allegory shrinkwraps the heroes and heroines of high tales as well as those stuck in the 'Field of Folk'" (172). He concludes: "allegory renders knowledge convenient, compressed, and compact" and "in the Enlightenment became an emblem of itself, an eternal process of repetition and expansion contained in the open, lively space between querying viewer and the cooperating—if confined—page" (211). In other words, the form mimics the conflict of the late seventeenth and early eighteenth-century postal system; on the one hand the system allows infinite expansion—an unending sequence of messages—while on the other hand it confines residents to designated mail routes, breaking communication between towns located close to one another geographically.

14. Robinson's pre-internet use of the web metaphor illustrates that even in the seventeenth century the delivery of the post was perceived as a uniquely complex and uncontrollable system with infinite possibility—an attitude that now characterizes public reaction to electronic mail.

15. The apocalyptic warning *is* public, in a sense, since it is written in a book to which all of the townspeople have access, but it remains a secret because the citizens do not read the book's pages.

16. The administrative position of secretary, in fact, is defined by its function as a repository of secret information.

17. Of course, Bunyan draws from scripture for precedent, recalling the community resistance faced by the major and minor prophets of the Old Testament.

18. My reading of the second part is not at odds with common critical reception, such as Frye's, in which Christiana, her children, Mercie, and Great-Heart represent communal responsibility in Christian life (145).

19. Even Evangelist, who hands Christian a parchment roll with the command, "Fly from the wrath to come," never reads the messages he passes on. Their dialogue also never confirms Christian's reading; Evangelist merely asks why he stays in the city if he is so certain of its eventual fall (9).

20. Christiana's exchange with the neighbor women may also provide evidence for a point Anderson makes about "national print-languages" when he states that "the convergence of capitalism and print technology on the fatal diversity of human language created the possibility of a new form of imagined community, which in its basic morphology set the stage for the modern nation" (Anderson 46). I do not discuss capitalism in my study and focus almost entirely on information technologies, though the two topics share several important connections. At the beginning of the second part, for example, the narrator remarks that he has been unable to inquire after Christian or his family because "the Multiplicity of Business" kept him away (143). Vanity Fair, of course, can also be read in terms of an early emerging capitalist spirit.

21. The sights in the Interpreter's House are displayed in secret rooms only accessible with the Interpreter as guide. As Swaim points out, the rooms are "opaque in surface, revelatory only to those who are in the house or have the Interpreter at hand, in other words the Elect" (86).

22. Davies calls Bunyan's interpretive exercises "lessons in a graceful hermeneutics" (7). "Graceful reading," Davies explains, is "a type of reading that involves more than an acknowledgement of the words on the page: it demands a particular kind of response and a strenuous one at that" (6–7).

23. Davies astutely points out that "it is the reader who is always the central focus of Bunyan's texts" (8).

24. My reading of Christiana and Mercie's reactions to the bodies of Simple, Sloth, and Presumption counters Sadler's reading of the women's reactions to the crucified body of Christ, in which she implies that the women and children are protected from unpleasant spectacles: "The women and children do not see the blood of the crucified Christ or the holes of the nails in the body; rather, from the top of the Wicket-Gate, they view the Crucifixion 'afar off'" (98). I argue instead that shocking spectacle becomes increasingly important for the women and children to see on their journey, from the hung bodies to the Giant Despair's decapitated head on a pole, because habitual reading threatens the discourse network of the Celestial City, which depends upon close reading, not reading from "'afar off." To challenge Christiana and her colleagues to read more closely, more attention-getting sights, like the new ones the Interpreter exhibits, are needed.

25. Critics refer to the signs along the way, which are sometimes left by Christian and Hopeful but also occasionally left by an anonymous author, differently depending upon the focus of their reading. Sharrock, who reads the second part of *Pilgrim's Progress* as a "conducted tour of former battlefields," sees the signs as "monuments to Christian's fights and sufferings," while Swaim looks to the "markers along the way" as Christian's way of "authoriz[ing] future reading and enfold[ing] these audiences into the dominant heroics" ("Women and Children" 175, Swaim 47).

26. Cunningham feels that the Doubting Castle episode "registers a haunting, lingering fear of *The Pilgrim's Progress* that the promises are always potentially miserable, misreadable, about to become null and void, that they might simply be absent when you most want them to be present" (229). Cunningham does not make the point, but the sign Christian and Hopeful erect at the edge of the giant's property, which is significantly a warning and not a promise, marks their attempt to prevent future misreading. Warnings in *Pilgrim's Progress* have the special ability to motivate characters along the way to the Celestial City, while promises are almost always suspicious and insincere.

27. Traditional readings of *Pilgrim's Progress* describe Christian's journey as the Puritan struggle through the five stages of progress toward God: election, vocation, justification, sanctification, and glorification (Bremer 20). Although I agree with these readings, I also maintain that the spatial representation of the struggle mimics a late seventeenth-century information system's concern with distance communication.

28. In "The Age of the World Picture," Heidegger explains that since the rise of the printing business, a published work can "bring the world into the picture for the public and confirm it publicly" (139).

NOTES TO CHAPTER TWO

1. Paxman reads *Oroonoko* with a similar strategy, though he locates conflicts between oral and written discourse, represented by native cultures and English imperialists respectively. He also links Behn's interest in the transition from oral to print communication with her own transition from drama to prose fiction (89). While, like Paxman, I am reading Behn's fiction in terms of contrasting discourses, I am not connecting either with particular characters, nor do I set the discourses in competition with one another.

2. See also Craft-Fairchild, who reads the *History* as a "subversive female story" (11).

3. Altaba-Artal counters Pearson's suggestion that the figures of nun and woman writer are metaphorically linked in the *History* and instead argues that Behn's belief in redemption is an "easier explanation" (156). Altaba-

Artal's focus is the dialogism of the *History* and *The Nun; or, The Perjur'd Beauty: A True Novel,* citing Behn's adaptation of multiple voices to create what Bakhtin dubs "heteroglossia." Significantly, Altaba-Artal's reading of the *History* gets the plot wrong, mistakenly identifying Villenoys as the husband who is misreported dead and omitting Henault. The misreading allows her to draw clearer parallels between Behn's novel and a similar work by María de Zayas y Sotomayor, an early seventeenth-century Spanish author, but it complicates her analysis and leads to simplification of the complexity of the *History.*

4. Spencer does, though, acknowledge that as the narrative progresses reader sympathy for Isabella grows, so that in the end the "novel resists easy moral interpretation" (172).

5. How calls the connections made possible by the Post Office "epistolary spaces," which he defines as "permanent and seemingly unbreakable links between people and ideas" (4).

6. My analysis of the link between transference of information and inheritance builds from Brooks's work on plot and Duyfhuizen's study of what he calls "narratives of transmission" (Duyfhuizen 16). Brooks looks more to the nineteenth-century novel when he asserts that "the problem of transmission" is at the core of plotting, which he suggests can be obviously seen in "the relations of fathers to sons (and also daughters to mothers, aunts, madwomen, and others), asking where an inheritable wisdom is to be found and how its transmission is to be acted toward" (27–8). Duyfhuizen takes Brooks's research a step further when he establishes transmission theory, which takes as its premise that "Western society depends on transmission, and especially textual transmission, to record and pass on legal codes, business records, marriage, birth, and property records" (27). Duyfhuizen is particularly interested in Brooks's alignment of plot with genealogical transmission of birthright, property, and money (41). Where my approach diverges from Brooks's study is in my focus first on the eighteenth-century novel and, second, on the impossible position of the female character within the circulation of messages and inheritance. What Brooks argues for the nineteenth-century novel—that it "seems to be inseparable from the conflict of movement and resistance, revolution and restoration, and from the issues of authority and paternity"—is true for Behn's novel as well. And in contrast to Duyfhuizen's work, my analysis does not look at framing devices or more obvious examples of narratives of transmission. For example, his study contains a chapter on the epistolary novel as a "textual society" (46). The *History* does not qualify as an epistolary narrative. In fact, I find its portrayal of textual transmission important for the purposes of studying late seventeenth-century information systems because letters do not consume or absolutely drive the narrative but subtly derail it, problematizing the relation between what would seem to be the main plot of the novel—Isabella's breaking of vows—and what emerges as a counterplot—misinformation by mail.

7. Though Isabella is not portrayed as an avid letter writer when she lives in the convent, she often visits the grate to talk with passers-by, which she mentions in a discussion with Katteriena (221). Walker finds that the grate was an important site of correspondence for nuns of the late seventeenth century: "Their personal experience was supplemented by news gleaned from visitors at the grate, and through letters" (162).

8. Even Isabella's function as an "example" for female readers follows this type of communication model. Isabella is set up by the narrator to be an example for female readers tempted to break their romantic vows. Eisenstein finds that, thanks to the explosion of communications networks, the "example" gained even more popularity as a means of improving personal behavior. She observes that the increased complexity of early modern information networks helped propel definitions of "ideal types" as "exactly repeatable pictoral statement[s]" (84). At the same time, citizens were also becoming fascinated with the possibility of a "sequence of corrupted copies" (4). Eisenstein's point is astute, yet the exemplary model for behavior did not originate out of or because of print culture. Classical and biblical examples are many, such as the virtuous rape victim Lucretia, Odysseus's faithful, patient wife Penelope, and the thrice-widowed grandmother of Christ, St. Ann. That print may have facilitated the over-production of examples, however, is an interesting possibility.

9. Wyrick finds in her analysis of *Oroonoko* that "language appears to attain truth value only when the value coincides with death," an observation that may also apply to the *History* (40).

10. The narrative voice changes from third-person commentary to first-person dialogue during scenes between the two women. Ballaster is interested in the narrative shift that occurs in the scene, from the impersonal third-person narration that is maintained throughout the novel to the more intimate first-person address to Katteriena. She concludes that direct speech "creates an illusion of immediacy that reported speech generally lacks" (72).

11. Isabella is not only upset that Katteriena has surprised her with the picture, but that she does so in an inappropriate place: the bedroom. Both the medium of the message and the timing and setting of the message, then, are problematic for Isabella.

12. What little readers learn about Katteriena is that her family forced her to take religious vows as punishment for a romantic relationship with her father's page (221). In other words, she was engaged in a romance forbidden because it crossed class lines that depend in part upon birthright to exist. By engaging in the affair with the page, Katteriena sacrifices her future birthright and, once her affair is discovered, her freedom.

13. Foreshadowing Henault's later reappearance after being pronounced dead, the dialogue also emphasizes his *return*, which has murderous connotations.

14. Upon joining the French army, Henault is contacted by Villenoys, who somehow receives word that Henault has reported to the same station. Even within the military camp, news travels fast.

15. Isabella, who bore false witness against her vow to serve God, is described similarly at the end of the novel when she is executed.

16. Henault's fear of breaking Isabella's picture parallels the theme of broken vows in the novel, and the fact that her picture is never broken could perhaps be read as evidence that, likewise, her vows are never truly broken either.

17. As in Lacan's analysis of the knock that wakes him from a nap, the sound seems to come from within a dream, and the subject's sleeping consciousness "reconstitutes itself around this representation of the knock" (56). From this point until the end of the novel, the narrative's tone is disoriented; the narrator withdraws from the retelling and never again offers a personal interpretation of the story.

18. The narrator does not speculate about what happened to those letters.

19. It is important to note that the murder scenes happen within the home. Carnell argues that "Behn reveals that true tragedies often occur in the private space of the household, a zone that she insists is artificially disconnected from and ignored by politically powerful, articulate men who control both government and the public sphere" (147). As the transmission of messages in the novel suggests, however, households since the development of the postal system are *not* totally disconnected.

20. It is not clear why Villenoys knocks on his own front door, unless it is because he was supposed to be on a hunting trip and returns prematurely, before anyone expects him, and is thus locked out of the house.

21. The false report thus begets more false reports.

22. Pearson spends time on the sewing metaphor in this scene, concluding that "needlework, conventionally an image of female subordination, becomes a locus of female power" and that "[s]uch paradoxes emphasize Isabella's ambiguous status as virtuous murderer, innocent adulteress" (248).

23. Not coincidentally, the *History* was published at the same time that newspapers underwent profound changes in their reporting practices. As McLuhan explains, early newspapers waited for news to come to them; in the era of Behn's writing, however, news writers learned how to create their own news events (212).

24. One reason Isabella confesses is because Villenoys's corpse opens its eyes and stares at her (256). Unlike the phantom of Henault, which is implied to be a hallucination, everyone present sees Villenoys's supernatural awakening.

25. Arguably, Isabella is doomed not because she breaks vows but because she makes too many of them.

26. I consider Isabella's address to her audience as it emphasizes, in Culler's words on apostrophe, "the circuit or situation of communication itself" rather than "meaning of a word" (135). Her speech, given from behind the

mourning veil, calls attention to the faceless exchange now possible because of developing information technologies (135).

NOTES TO CHAPTER THREE

1. As Traugott points out, the crowd image is "the organizing allegorical metaphor of the whole of the *Tale*" (157). Hammond notes that the *Tale* is a "satire on the current state of bookmaking," while Higgins recognizes it as "an artifact of modern print culture (83, 28).

2. Craven would disagree with Francus on the particulars of this point and argue that quantity and quality share a cause-and-effect relationship for the narrator: "The satiric voice in the *Tale* sees a profound qualitative information loss as a result of the information explosion" (154).

3. In the "Digression Concerning the Original, the Use, and the Improvement of Madness in a Commonwealth," the plural "informations" appears in the following context: "so far preferable is that wisdom that converses about the surface, to that pretended philosophy which enters into the depth of things, and then comes gravely back with the informations and discoveries that in the inside they are good for nothing" (83).

4. Montag goes further to observe that the *Tale* demonstrates "a playing of philosophical positions against each other in the absence of a secure theoretical terrain to defend" (91). The crowd's competitive spirit, then, parallels the general lack of collaboration between the scientists, philosophers, and writers of Swift's era.

5. Karian studies the ways in which Swift's work was compiled and marketed in the eighteenth century. As he considers patterns of omission and modification in contemporary anthologies, he uses the term "paratext," a concept he borrows from Gerard Genette, to describe those material inclusions (peritext) or additions to (epitext) a text, such as the title page, preface, apology, and footnotes. I also use the term to refer to the intertextual elements of Swift's *Tale*.

6. Critics have commented often on the impossibility of pinning Swift down to any one opinion. Fox remarks, for example, that Swift had "an uncanny ability to become what he attacked and then borrow from within" (1). McMinn writes that the "parasitical nature of parody ensured that many readers would identify and confuse the beliefs within the text with those of the author" (20). Mueller notes that "the *Tale's* narrator is not a consistent persona but rather the shifting expression of a *mélange* of perspectives, some of them Swift's, some of them targets of derision" (208).

7. Recognizing the constructive goals of the *Tale* answers, in part, an invitation by Suarez to focus less on the "destructive elements" of the work (115).

8. What Swift's catalog does not include, however, because it lists only books, are the numerous correspondences he must have read and mediated for

Temple. A good deal of his knowledge of "dark, mysterious writings," as Hammond calls them, may actually have come from his reading and writing of letters (79).

9. Reddick sees Swift's use of the body as bound by his perspective on wit: "Swift plays with the earlier notions of wit as the function of discovery and seeing into, allied with clarity and quickness" (161).

10. Rushworth asks for an approach of this nature, since he believes that "what has been lost to criticism of the *Tale* is an appreciation of the precariousness of its physical form commensurate with the appreciation of the general uncertainty of the *Tale's* meaning" (43).

11. As is characteristic of the narrator, readers cannot know how seriously he takes this solution, because the suggestion appears in a section that celebrates digression.

12. When Swift grants his readers permission to move his digression on digressions to another "corner," he concedes that readers do still look past titles and indexes (though the *Tale* lacks the latter) to consider the body of the text (72).

13. Ezell finds in her study of print at the end of the seventeenth century and the beginning of the eighteenth century that the narrator's fear was premature. "There was not a noticeable boom in printing literary texts immediately after the expiration of the licensing act," she writes; "getting into print in the seventeenth and early eighteenth centuries for the majority of writers who deliberately sought out the new mode of authorship still involved lengthy negotiations by the author with several different individual technicians at different stages of production" (111, 86).

14. Works of media theory in the late twentieth century exhibit a similar apocalyptic turn, as I will discuss in the conclusion to this study.

15. In the apology, the narrator responds to criticism of the *Tale*, much of which accuses him of plagiarism. For example, one "answerer," as he calls his critics, claims that "the names of Peter, Martin, and Jack, are borrowed from a Letter of the late Duke of Buckingham" (6). The narrator denies ever hearing of such a letter. The accusation raises the question of where the distinction lies between collection and plagiarism. Between the apology and the *Tale* itself he indicates that the two practices are indeed different, but he provides no explanation as to how. At one moment he may openly admit that he has "just come from perusing some hundreds of prefaces" and proceed to copy out phrases from them, but at another he "insists upon it that through the whole book he has not borrowed one single hint from any writer in the world" (20, 6).

16. Ong's observation can be interpreted in at least two other ways, of course, both relevant to Swift's *Tale*. First, the emergence of new genres of writing, like the commonplace book and the news report, "mobilize knowledge" as seemingly straightforward objective information. Second, Ong is also

describing the transition from an oral culture, in which travelling story-tellers move knowledge from place to place in narrative form, to a print culture, in which mass media like print can pass knowledge on more quickly and more easily. Though carriers or travelling citizens are still important in the mobilization of knowledge in print, they play a less central role in the communication, interpretation and dissemination of material.

17. Connections between the *Tale's* presentation of information overload and the twentieth- and twenty-first-century technological situations are plentiful. Craven ends his first chapter in a worried tone, noting that today "probing beneath the surface has become a viable, if still discomfiting option" and wondering whether "twenty-first-century Europe will live on with the irreplaceable legacy of Venetian art or the inundating pollution of Venetian commerce" (16). Though I agree that there are parallels between the internet and early print cultures as surface-centric, environmentally and intellectually wasteful systems, I want to avoid drawing hasty comparisons between two ages that are otherwise so very different. My references to twenty-first-century technological, social, or intellectual environments will operate only as analogies or frames of reference to help readers better understand an eighteenth-century perspective.

18. Montag goes so far as to adopt the narrator's language in his own analysis. Claiming that scholars will not get far trying to conduct close readings of the *Tale,* he argues that we instead "move from inside the works to the outside, that which makes them what they are and no other, the conditions of their singular existence" (3).

19. The pattern of reversal and negation that Swift imitates creates what Lèvy would call a "Moebius effect" (*Becoming* 33).

20. Ehrenpreis speculates, in his third volume of the author's biography, that Swift's descriptions of the human body may be explained by a childhood discomfort with bodily process (466). I acknowledge the psychoanalytic possibilities here, but I believe that Swift's bodily descriptions of textual multiplicity are part of a larger metaphorical trend in the etymological history of information.

21. The question of why and how collections and the act of collecting facilitate readers' appropriation of ideas not their own may help us better understand plagiarism in the twenty-first-century writing classroom. While the argument that plagiarism is always intentional, that writers should always be able to identify their own ideas from those they adopted from another, has been a convincing one in pedagogical circles, it also may be worth exploring more closely the common claim that some acts of plagiarism result from the writer's complete internalization of another's ideas, that "unintentional" plagiarism is more complicated than has been assumed. Do certain forms of writing, like collections, increase the possibility that a writer will forget from where or whom an idea came? Does the very structure of a compila-

tion work in some way against the social conventions that writers are expected to follow in their own writing?

22. While Swift's attacks on writers, politicians, religious figures, and scientists have been much commented on by critics including Bloom, Rawson, Boyle, and Traugott, his use of defamation as narrative strategy has not yet been addressed.

23. Craven believes that the "key metaphor, a tub, describes a systems program designed to keep moderns preoccupied with surfaces" (7). I agree, but I do not think that Swift necessarily wishes his readers to be "preoccupied with surfaces." Rather, I argue that he uses the tub and other metaphors, as well as the practice of defamation, as self-conscious strategies that depend upon a balance of publicity and secrecy to be effective.

24. "Glancing anxiously and repeatedly from text to footnote, the reader may come to feel that he or she has been led into a ritual display of ignorance," Bogel claims, "and that the text has maneuvered its readers into a position uncomfortably like that occupied by the figures it satirizes, a position of duncical incompetence" (27–8).

25. Craven would agree with Griffin on this point, believing that Swift has, in fact, successfully tricked generations of critics into reading the *Tale* on the surface: "Certain that modern commentators of the *Tale* would go helter-skelter in all directions, Swift even concocted a global information-analysis project of his own, a modern game plan, to insure that all modern critics, the putative commentators, would gather about the tub at its evanescent surface" (15).

26. By continually adding material to the beginning of the work—treatise, apology to the reader, and dedication to Somers—the author also demonstrates textual "wandering" on a structural level, since his responses to various accusations and bookseller errors actually *proceed* those accusations and errors. In the arrangement of the *Tale,* the prompt and the response intersect nonlinearly.

27. Higgins sees the *Tale's* spiral into insanity as a satirical reenactment of Locke's conclusion that imagination unrestrained will cause the subject to break down, overcome by madness (28).

28. For example, the narrator writes: "Now this disappointment (to discover a secret) I must own gave me the first hint of setting up for an author" (103).

29. Epstein has developed a number of online venues, such as *InteLnet,* "Collective Improvisations," and "ThinkLinks," which strive to create a "megamind" of creative interdisciplinary ideas about culture, literature, philosophy, and other subjects (*Who* 6). These sites encourage thinking through association, inspiring submissions that much resemble moments in the *Tale;* for example, online message boards allow multiple authors to post their own fragmented ideas and build upon previous participants' ideas, which creates a narrative organized similarly to the *Tale's* metaphorical lists.

NOTES TO CHAPTER FOUR

1. One week after the World Trade Center bombings, a similar message was transmitted about a suspected e-mail virus: "VIRUS writers have circulated a computer virus purporting to be information about the World Trade Center. The virus, dubbed "WTC," [sic] is a version of the LifeStages virus, which crashed computer systems around the world in June last year" (Colwell 1). The message ends by stating: "Please practice safe computing. Don't open unsolicited attachments. Don't let these creeps take advantage of the raw emotion surrounding the events of the last few weeks" (1).

2. Novak sees *Due Preparations* and the *Journal* as serving two different purposes: the first to help readers reconcile the plague with their religious beliefs and the latter to offer readers a "fantasy of escape" (*Master* 603). Both works, Moore finds, were timely and much welcomed by a public that "had already proved receptive to works purporting to present lived experience" (136).

3. "It is hard for the modern reader to appreciate the eighteenth-century affection for public documents," Backscheider finds, and "[r]oyal proclamations, memorials, acts, and speeches were routinely printed by the printer holding the royal patent; these same publications were reprinted, usually in their entirety, in periodicals, in annuals, and in books like Defoe's" (*Ambition* 98).

4. I am not arguing that Defoe's writings mark the first or earliest points at which a medium, whether oral or print, constitute a virtualization of a historical event, nor am I arguing that the event must be traumatic, individually or collectively, in order to trigger perpetual, obsessive record-keeping to the extent that the plague does. I am building from Lèvy's study of the virtualization of bodies and texts in the modern media state.

5. Lèvy's definition of virtual reality is very similar to the reality that H.F. describes in his journal. The virtual state, Lèvy discovers, is one in which there is increased focus on circulation, on the transportation of things inside and out of the body (40).

6. The first lines of the *Journal* change depending upon the edition. These lines are from the first edition of 1722, the only edition to be published while Defoe was alive and, therefore, the edition used for this reading. A comparison of the 1722 edition with later ones edited and, apparently, rewritten by other hands, reveals striking differences in focus and in certainty. The first version reflects an obvious concern with the movement of news about the returning plague, but the second edition of 1763 omits Defoe's description of rumor and discourse and instead focuses on the agency of God. The 1763 version also turns to religion and providence. The 1795 version makes sure to state the origin: "This dreadful contagion in London was introduced by some goods brought from Holland" (1).

7. H.F.'s journey through the city to compile anecdotes about the plague experience is very similar to Defoe's own journeys as a spy in the summer of 1704, when he sends reports to Robert Harley, Secretary of State for the Northern Division. According to Backscheider, Defoe "generally limited himself to reporting his observations, interpreting them in a sentence or two, and shipping brief recommendations into the reports" (*His Life* 159–60).

8. Wainwright, like Earle, focuses on the situation of the poor in the work and sees the *Journal* as a rhetorical attempt to persuade contemporary readers to reconsider their attitudes toward and sympathy for the poor (60).

9. The point here is not to criticize methods used by public health officials to identify and organize information about infectious diseases but to argue that the visual presentation of the plague in the bills, however necessary for future prevention, reflects a larger organizing pattern present in H.F.'s media state.

10. Blanchot actually uses the word "cancer" in his description, but in the preceding line he acknowledges that leprosy and plague work in the same way (87).

11. Blanchot's point is not difficult for twenty-first century readers to imagine, since programs are some of the first targets of computer viruses, which work much like biological contaminants. Eighteenth-century readers, however, had no access to so fitting an analogy.

12. H.F.'s anonymity, of course, is also a type of secret.

13. Starr notes that H.F. presents a "series of questions to be answered" (56).

14. Again, the similarities between plague-time London and twentieth and twenty-first century encounters with terrorism are striking. The media after September 11 immediately focused on the terrorist's ability to enter and exit the United States, pointing to the country's multiple entryways and wide accessibility as points of vulnerability. President George W. Bush's "Operation Homeland Security" adopts the home as symbol of a tightly contained space shut off from foreign invasion by parties that can move, like invisible contaminants, back and forth across national borders. As in the *Journal,* vulnerable national boundaries are referred to metaphorically as domestic ones; trespassing on residential private property represents foreign movement across U.S. airspace and soil.

15. Though he does not develop the point further, Richetti makes an astute observation when he notes that the *Journal* introduces "a world of unprecedented quantities" (120).

16. Not long before the 1665 plague, Leeuwenhoek and Hooke observed microscopic creatures in saliva and blood that were thought to be connected to the disease.

17. Various critics have noticed Defoe's use of the house as symbol in the *Journal.* Warner, for example, points out that the "house symbolism in the *Journal* can be related to similar symbolism in Defoe's fiction. There is a

compulsive use of imagery of containment, along with a very deep ambivalence about containment" (46). Warner argues, however, that the home is "a reflection of Defoe's ambivalence toward the isolation of myth. For H.F. the house stands as a safe retreat, but only if he is willing to forswear involvement in history. For a time, he does so, only to return to the observation of society" (46).

18. The horrors on the other side of his windowpane, using Blanchot's words, have "the imperceptible but intense suddenness of the outside" (4).

19. Stephanson reaches a similar conclusion, remarking that "Defoe expertly dramatizes imaginative restriction and paralysis through physical confinement—a 'Neighbourhood of Walls'" (234).

20. Like the job of the night watchman, H.F.'s occupations both before and during the plague are fitting in light of the *Journal's* emphasis on global communication and the blurred boundary between the exchange and the message. H.F. works as a saddler, a tradesman who sells supplies to travelers and makes much of his money overseas in the developing North American colonies—colonies that were being reterritorialized and that developed, many thought lawlessly, out of sight of London officials who were uncertain how to apply and enforce policy. His business, in a sense, is the blurred boundary. During the plague, H.F. is "assigned by the government to be an official examiner for the city's public health work" (11). In this role he, like the watchman, is charged with the task of witnessing individual suffering without responding to it.

21. Blanchot's thoughts on witnessing are helpful for understanding the context of the watchman, particularly when he describes a "distantness that keeps watch beyond attention" and that is "neither negative nor positive, but excessive, which is to say without intentionality, without reproval" (Blanchot 55). The watchman must also witness in excess and suspend judgement on what he sees and hears. His presence, though, is both positive and negative, since his job is, on the one hand, to save the lives of the uninfected and to help the infected who are contained in the home by delivering food and supplies and, on the other hand, to imprison the healthy with the sick in case of previous exposure. As enforcers of the policy for shutting up houses, which H.F. views as more of an order of death than a law for survival, the watchman also "refers endlessly to a dead law which in its very fall, fails yet again, the lawless law of death" (Blanchot 55).

22. The moment marks what Laub would call the "mutual recognition of a shared knowledge" (64). Backscheider arrives at a similar conclusion about the *Journal,* stating that it "arrests a moment of collective consciousness" (*Ambition* 135).

23. Similarly, in the hours after the September 11 bombings, when internet news sites like CNN.com were overloaded with users, citizens turned to chat rooms in unprecedented numbers; residents of New York City reported

what they saw out their windows; others reached the same conclusions that would gradually emerge in television reports during the next few weeks. *New York Times* reporter Amy Harmon writes, on September 12, that "Amateur news reporters on weblogs are functioning as their own decentralized media today."

24. It is not clear whether H.F. dies of the plague, which has abated by the end of the journal or, as is more likely, he dies of some other ailment some time after the journal is written but before it is printed.

25. The close of the journal seems not to be a conventional ending at all, but is rather the point at which H.F., in his own words, "can go no farther" (248). As Langer might say, "his narrative emerges not as a story of survival, but of deprival" (16). Langer also writes that "Individual 'successes' are invariably tainted by the conjunction, 'I'm alive,'" which he feels "simply lacks the moral resonance of 'I survived'" (23). H.F.'s last words are, interestingly, not "I survived" but "yet I alive." Backscheider interprets the last words very differently than I do: "His experience, begun in pious questioning, ends in gratitude for his life but not in answers. Just as the huge growth of domestic manufacture and trade transformed England, so did the memoirs of men who survived the fire" (*Ambition* 142). Birdsall ends her study of the *Journal* with H.F.'s last words, "And I Alive," but she does not offer a reading of the statement.

NOTES TO THE AFTERWORD

1. Surprisingly, in an essay on "The Work of Walter Benjamin in the Age of Information," Noah Isenberg never mentions Benjamin's critique of the concept in "The Storyteller." Ironically, Isenberg instead focuses on the way in which Benjamin, whose short essays, vignettes, and "poignant aphorisms" have become popular sources for twenty-first-century theorists, is "intrinsically appealing in view of the demands for abbreviation in this age of information" (123).

2. See Davis's convincing argument about the novel's claims of historical truth in *Factual Fictions: The Origins of the English Novel* (1983).

3. As Hesse argues in the case of digital technology, the spirit of experimentation found in the works of Bunyan, Behn, Swift, and Defoe may have less to do with technological innovation than with institutional practices of regulation. Hesse writes of today's literary situation that the "kind of experimentation that we are currently witnessing in electronic publication is a symptom of an underregulated or rather, relative to print media, unregulated communications medium that has evolved alongside of or beyond the reach of current regulatory frameworks" (28).

4. As has been discussed in several studies of Habermas, communication is central to his theory (Zipes 94).

5. Barker argues that the identity of "the public" in the mid- and late-eighteenth century is debatable: "For some, it described those whose constitutional standing, education or wealth gave them a legitimate say in the nation's affairs; for others, the term was synonymous with the mob" (94).

6. My discussion of the "cultural environment" of media follows Heise's characterization of twentieth- and twenty-first-century theory. Heise is most concerned with environmental and ecological metaphors used to describe information, but her categories sketch a useful general picture of the theoretical direction of scholarly discussions of the subject.

Bibliography

Abraham, N. "Notes on the Phantom: A Complement to Freud's Metapsychology." Trans. N. Rand. *Critical Inquiry.* 13 (1987): 287–92.

Ainsworth, William Harrison. *Old Saint Paul's: A Tale of the Plague and the Fire.* London: Routledge, 1841.

Alliston, April. *Virtue's Faults: Correspondence in Eighteenth-Century British and French Women's Fiction.* Stanford: Stanford UP, 1996.

Altaba-Artal, Dolors. *Aphra Behn's English Feminism: Wit and Satire.* Selinsgrove: Susquehanna UP, 1999.

Anderson, Benedict. *Imagined Communities: Reflections on the Origin and Spread of Nationalism.* London: Verso, 1991.

Arendt, Hannah. *Between Past and Future: Six Exercises in Political Thought.* New York: Viking, 1961.

Backscheider, Paula R. *Daniel Defoe: Ambition and Innovation.* Lexington: UP of Kentucky, 1986.

———. *Daniel Defoe: His Life.* Baltimore: The Johns Hopkins UP, 1989.

Ballaster, Rosalind. *Seductive Forms: Women's Amatory Fiction from 1684–1740.* Oxford: Clarendon, 1992.

Barker, Hannah. "England, 1760–1815." *Press, Politics, and the Public Sphere in Europe and North America, 1760–1820.* Ed. Hannah Barker and Simon Burrows. Cambridge: Cambridge UP, 2002. 93–112.

Baudrillard, Jean. *Simulacra and Simulation.* Trans. Sheila Faria Glaser. Ann Arbor: U of Michigan P, 1994.

Behn, Aphra. *The History of the Nun: or, The Fair Vow-Breaker.* 1798. *The Works of Aphra Behn, Vol. 3: The Fair Jilt and Other Stories.* Ed. Janet Todd. Columbus: Ohio State UP, 1995.

Bell, Daniel. *The Coming of the Post-Industrial Society.* New York: Basic Books, 1973.

Bell, Walter George. *The Great Plague in London in 1665.* London: John Lane the Bodley Head Ltd., 1924.

Benjamin, Walter. "The Storyteller." *Illuminations.* Ed. Hannah Arendt. Trans. Harry Zohn. New York: Schocken, 1969. 83–109.

Birdsall, Virginia Ogden. *Defoe's Perpetual Seekers: A Study of the Major Fiction.* Lewisburg: Bucknell UP, 1985.

Blanchard, W. Scott. "Swift's *Tale*, the Renaissance Anatomy, and Humanist Polemic." *Representations of Swift.* Ed. Brian A. Connery. Newark: U of Delaware P, 2002. 57–73.

Blanchot, Maurice. *The Writing of Disaster.* Trans. Ann Smock. Lincoln: U of Nebraska P, 1995.

Bloom, Harold. Introduction to *Modern Critical Views: Jonathan Swift.* Ed. Harold Bloom. New York: Chelsea House, 1986. 1–11.

Bogel, Fredric V. *The Difference Satire Makes: Rhetoric and Reading from Jonson to Byron.* Ithaca: Cornell UP, 2001.

Bolter, David J. *Writing Space: The Computer, Hypertext, and the History of Writing.* Hillsdale, NJ: L. Erlbaum, 1991.

Boyle, Frank. *Swift as Nemesis: Modernity and its Satirist.* Stanford: Stanford UP, 2000.

Breen, Margaret Soenser. "Christiana's Rudeness: Spiritual Authority in *The Pilgrim's Progress.*" *Bunyan Studies.* 7 (1997): 96–111.

Bremer, Francis J. *The Puritan Experiment: New England Society from Bradford to Edwards.* Hanover : UP of New England, 1995.

Bristol, Michael D. and Marotti, Arthur F. Introduction to *Print, Manuscript, and Performance: The Changing Relations of the Media in Early Modern England.* Ed. Arthur F. Marotti and Michael D. Bristol. Columbus: Ohio State UP, 2000. 1–29.

Brooks, Peter. *Reading for the Plot: Design and Intention in Narrative.* New York: Alfred A. Knopf, 1984.

Brown, Sylvia. "The Reproductive Word: Gender and Textuality in the Writings of John Bunyan." *Bunyan Studies.* 11 (2003–2004): 23–45.

Browne, Christopher. *Getting the Message: The Story of the British Post Office.* Dover: Sutton, 1993.

Bruster, Douglas. "The Structural Transformation of Print in Late Elizabethan England." *Print, Manuscript and Performance: The Changing Relations of the Media in Early Modern England.* Ed. Arthur F. Marotti and Michael D. Bristol. Columbus: Ohio State UP, 2000. 49–89.

Bunyan, John. *The Pilgrim's Progress.* 1678. Ed. N.H. Keeble. Oxford: Oxford UP, 1984.

Calder, Nigel. *The Comet is Coming!: The Feverish Legacy of Mr. Halley.* New York: Viking P, 1980.

Capurro, Rafael. "On the Genealogy of Information." *Information: New Questions to a Multidisciplinary Concept.* Eds. Klaus Kornwachs and Konstantin Jacoby. Berlin: Akademie Verlag, 1996. 259–270.

Carnell, Rachel K. "Subverting Tragic Convention: Aphra Behn's Turn to the Novel." *Studies in the Novel.* 31 (1999): 133–151.

Colwell, Wanda Sue. "FW: Virus Targets Attack Victims." E-mail to slastaff@list-serv.iupui.edu. 19 September 2001.

Cope, Kevin L. *Enlightening Allegory: Theory, Practice and Contexts of Allegory in the Late Seventeenth and Eighteenth Centuries.* New York: AMS, 1993.

Corporation of London. *London's Dreadful Visitation: or, A Collection of All the Bills of Mortality for This Present Year: Beginning the 20th of December 1664 and Ending the 19th of December Following.* London, 1665.

Craft-Fairchild, Catherine. *Masquerade and Gender: Disguise and Female Identity in Eighteenth-Century Fictions by Women.* University Park: Pennsylvania State UP, 1993.

Craven, Kenneth. *Jonathan Swift and the Millennium of Madness: The Information Age in Swift's A Tale of a Tub.* London: E.J. Brill, 1992.

Crawford, Susan. "The Origin and Development of a Concept: The Information Society." *Bulletin of the Medical Library Association.* 7.4 (1983): 380–5.

Crime Prevention List. "Suspicious Package Checklist." E-mail to police-1@listserv.cc.emory.edu. 16 October 2001.

Culler, Jonathan. *The Pursuit of Signs: Semiotics, Literature, Deconstruction.* Ithaca: Cornell UP, 1981.

Cunningham, Valentine. "Glossing and Glozing: Bunyan and Allegory." *John Bunyan Conventicle and Parnassus: Tercentenary Essays.* Ed. N.H. Keeble. Oxford: Clarendon, 1988. 217–240.

Daiches, David. *A Critical History of English Literature: The Restoration to 1800.* Vol. III. London: Secker and Warburg, 1960.

Davies, Michael. *Graceful Reading: Theology and Narrative in the Works of John Bunyan.* Oxford: Oxford UP, 2002.

Davis, Lennard. *Factual Fictions: The Origins of the English Novel.* New York: Columbia UP, 1983.

Daybell, James. Introduction to *Early Modern Women's Letter Writing, 1450–1700.* Ed. James Daybell. New York: Palgrave, 2001.

Deeming, David. "The Tale, Temple, and Swift's Irish Aesthetic." *Representations of Swift.* Ed. Brian A. Connery. Newark: U of Delaware P, 2002. 25–40.

Defoe, Daniel. *A Journal of the Plague Year.* 1722. Oxford: Oxford UP, 1990.

——. *Due Preparations for the Plague, as Well for Soul as Body: Being Some Seasonable Thoughts Upon the Visible Approach of the Present Dreadful Contagion in France.* 1722. Boston: David Nickerson, Co., 1903.

——. *The Storm: or, A Collection of the Most Remarkable Casualties and Disasters Which Happen'd in the Late Dreadful Tempest, Both by Sea and Land.* London, 1704.

Deleuze, Gilles and Félix Guattari. *A Thousand Plateaus: Capitalism and Schizophrenia.* Trans. Brian Massumi. Minneapolis: U of Minnesota P, 1987.

De Marco, Nick. "Structural 'Pliability' and Narratological 'Diffidence' in *The Pilgrim's Progress.*" *Bunyan Studies.* 8 (1998): 36–53.

DePorte, Michael. "Flinging It All Out of the Windows: The 'Digression on Madness.'" *Critical Approaches to Teaching Swift.* Ed. Peter J. Schakel. New York: AMS P, 1992. 174–183.

Donovan, Josephine. *Women and the Rise of the Novel, 1405–1726.* New York: St. Martin, 1999.

Doyle, Richard. "LSDNA: Consciousness Expansion and the Emergence of Biotechnology." *Data Made Flesh: Embodying Information.* Ed. Robert Mitchell and Phillip Thurtle. New York: Routledge, 2004. 103–120.

Duff, Alistair S. *Information Society Studies.* New York: Routledge, 2000.

Dupuy, Jean-Pierre. "Myths of the Informational Society." *The Myths of Information: Technology and Postindustrial Culture.* Ed. Kathleen Woodward. Madison: Coder P, 1980. 3–17.

Duyfhuizen, Bernard. *Narratives of Transmission.* Cranbury: Associated UP, 1992.

Earle, Peter. *The World of Defoe.* London: Weidenfeld and Nicolson, 1976.

Ehrenpreis, Irvin. *Swift: The Man, His Works, and the Age.* 3 vols. London: Methuen, 1962–83.

Eisenstein, Elizabeth L. *The Printing Press as an Agent of Change: Communications and Cultural Transformations in Early Modern Europe.* New York: Cambridge UP, 1979.

Ellis, Frank. "No Apologies, Dr. Swift!" *Eighteenth-Century Life.* 21 (November 1997): 71–76.

Ellis, Kenneth. *The Post Office in the Eighteenth Century: A Study in Administrative History.* London: Oxford UP, 1958.

Epstein, Mikhail. "Collective Improvisations." *InteLnet.* July 1995. <http://www.emory.edu/INTELNET/impro_home.html >.

——. *Who I Am and Why I Decided to Start Intelnet.* 23 Oct. 1995 <http://www.emory.edu/INTELNET/Who_I_and_why_Intelnet.html.>

——. "ThinkLinks." *InteLnet.* July 1995. < http://comm.cudenver.edu /~inteLnet/cgi-bin/ThinkLinks.html>.

Ezell, Margaret J.M. *Social Authorship and the Advent of Print.* Baltimore: Johns Hopkins UP, 1999.

Fabricant, Carole. "Swift the Irishman." *The Cambridge Companion to Jonathan Swift.* Ed. Christopher Fox. Cambridge: Cambridge UP, 2003. 48–72.

Fish, Stanley. *Self-Consuming Artifacts: The Experience of Seventeenth-Century Literature.* Berkeley: U of California P, 1972.

Flynn, Carol Houlihan. *The Body in Swift and Defoe.* Cambridge: Cambridge UP, 1990.

Fox, Christopher. Introduction to *The Cambridge Companion to Jonathan Swift.* Ed. Christopher Fox. Cambridge: Cambridge UP, 2003. 1–13.

Francus, Marilyn. *The Converting Imagination: Linguistic Theory and Swift's Satiric Prose.* Carbondale: Southern Illinois UP, 1994.

Frye, R.M. "The Way of All Pilgrims." 1960. *Bunyan's The Pilgrim's Progress: A Casebook.* Ed. Roger Sharrock. London: Macmillan, 1976. 144–157.

Gouldner, Alvin. *The Dialectic of Ideology and Technology.* New York: Oxford UP, 1982.

Graham, Jean. "'Tell All Men': Bunyan and the Gendering of Discourse." *Bunyan Studies.* 11 (2003–2004): 8–22.

Greaves, Richard L. "Conscience, Liberty, and the Spirit: Bunyan and Noncomformity." *John Bunyan Conventicle and Parnassus: Tercentenary Essays.* Ed. N.H. Keeble. Oxford: Clarendon, 1988. 21–43.

Griffin, Dustin. *Satire: A Critical Reintroduction.* Lexington: UP of Kentucky, 1994.

Habermas, Jürgen. *The Structural Transformation of the Public Sphere: An Inquiry into a Category of Bourgeois Society.* Trans. Thomas Burger. Cambridge: MIT P, 1989.

Hammond, Brean. "Swift's Reading." *The Cambridge Companion to Jonathan Swift.* Ed. Christopher Fox. Cambridge: Cambridge UP, 2003. 73–86.

Hancock, Maxine. "Identity, Agency and Community: Intimations and Implications of Emerging Literacy for Women in *The Pilgrim's Progress, The Second Part.*" *Bunyan Studies.* 11 (2003–2004): 74–93.

Harmon, Amy. "A Day of Terror: The Talk Online; Web Offers Both News and Comfort," *New York Times on the Web* 12 September 2001. 8 June 2003 http://www.nytimes.com/.

Hayles, N. Katherine, ed. *Chaos Bound: Orderly Disorder in Contemporary Literature and Science.* Ithaca: Cornell UP, 1990.

——. *Chaos and Order: Complex Dynamics in Literature and Science.* Chicago: U of Chicago P, 1991.

Healy, Margaret. "Defoe's *Journal* and the English Plague Writing Tradition." *Literature and Medicine.* 22.1 (2003): 25–44.

Heidegger, Martin. *The Question Concerning Technology, and Other Essays.* Trans. William Lovitt. New York: Harper, 1977.

Heise, Ursula K. "Unnatural Ecologies: The Metaphor of the Environment in Media Theory." *Configurations.* 10.1 (2002): 149–168.

Hemmeon, Joseph Clarence. *The History of the British Post Office.* Cambridge: Harvard UP, 1912.

Hesse, Carla. "Books in Time." *The Future of the Book.* Ed. Geoffrey Nunberg. Berkeley: U of California P, 1996. 21–36.

Higgins, Ian. *Jonathan Swift.* Horndon, UK: Northcote House P, 2004.

Hofmeyr, Isabel. *The Portable Bunyan: A Transnational History of The Pilgrim's Progress.* Princeton: Princeton UP, 2004.

Holly, Grant. "The Allegory in Realism." *Enlightening Allegory: Theory, Practice and Contexts of Allegory in the Late Seventeenth and Eighteenth Centuries.* Ed. Kevin L. Cope. New York: AMS, 1993. 131–69.

How, James. *Epistolary Spaces: English Letter Writing from the Foundation of the Post Office to Richardson's Clarissa.* Aldershot: Ashgate, 2003.

Isenberg, Noah. "The Work of Walter Benjamin in the Age of Information." *New German Critique: An Interdisciplinary Journal of German Studies.* 83 (2001): 119–50.

Juengel, Scott J. "Writing Decomposition: Defoe and the Corpse." *The Journal of Narrative Technique.* 25.2 (1995): 139–153.

Karian, Stephen. "Problems and Paratexts in Eighteenth-Century Collections of Swift." *Studies in Literary Imagination.* 32.1 (1999): 59–80.

Kaufmann, U. Milo. "Spiritual Discerning: Bunyan and the Mysteries of the Divine Will." *John Bunyan Conventicle and Parnassus: Tercentenary Essays.* Ed. N.H. Keeble. Oxford: Clarendon, 1988. 171–187.

Keeble, N.H. "Christiana's Key: The Unity of *The Pilgrim's Progress.*" *The Pilgrim's Progress: Critical and Historical Views.* Ed. Vincent Newey. Totowa: Barnes and Noble, 1980. 1–20.

Kernan, Alvin. *The Death of Literature.* New Haven: Yale UP, 1990.

Kittler, Friedrich. *Discourse Networks 1800/1900.* Trans. Michael Metteer. Stanford: Stanford UP, 1990.

———. *Gramophone, Film, Typewriter.* Trans. Geoffrey Winthrop-Young and Michael Wutz. Stanford: Stanford UP, 1999.

Klapp, Orrin E. *Overload and Boredom: Essays on the Quality of Life in the Information Society.* New York: Greenwood P, 1986.

Knox, Ronald. *Essays in Satire.* London: Sheed and Ward, 1928.

Lacan, Jacques. *The Four Fundamental Concepts of Psychoanalysis.* Trans. Alan Sheridan. New York: Norton, 1977.

———. *The Psychoses.* Trans. Russell Grigg. New York: Norton, 1993.

Langer, Lawrence. *Versions of Survival: The Holocaust and the Human Spirit.* Albany: State U of New York P, 1982.

Laub, Dori. "Bearing Witness or the Vicissitudes of Listening." *Testimony : Crises of Witnessing in Literature, Psychoanalysis, and History.* New York : Routledge, 1992. 57–74.

Levinas, Emmanuel. *Basic Philosophical Writings.* Ed. Adriaan T. Peperzak, Simon Critchley, and Robert Bernasconi. Bloomington: Indiana UP, 1996.

Lèvy, Pierre. *Becoming Virtual: Reality in the Digital Age.* Trans. Robert Bononno. New York: Plenum, 1998.

———. *Collective Intelligence: Mankind's Emerging World in Cyberspace.* Trans. Robert Bononno. New York: Plenum, 1997.

Locke, John. *An Essay Concerning Human Understanding.* (1689) Ed. Roger Woolhouse. New York: Penguin, 1997.

Lynch, Beth. *John Bunyan and the Language of Conviction.* Cambridge: D.S. Brewer, 2004.

Machlup, Fritz. *The Production and Distribution of Knowledge in the United States.* Princeton: Princeton UP, 1962.

Marvin, Carolyn. "Information and History." *The Ideology of the Information Age.* Ed. J.D. Slack and F. Fejes. Norwood, NJ: Ablex, 1987. 49–62.

May, Christopher. *The Information Society: A Sceptical View.* Cambridge: Polity P, 2002.

McLuhan, Marshall. *The Gutenberg Galaxy: The Making of Typographic Man.* Toronto: U of Toronto P, 1962.

———. *Understanding Media: The Extensions of Man.* New York: McGraw, 1964.

McMinn, Joseph. "Swift's Life." *The Cambridge Companion to Jonathan Swift.* Ed. Christopher Fox. Cambridge: Cambridge UP, 2003. 14–30.

Miles, Ian. "The New Post-Industrial State." *Futures.* 17.6 (1985): 588–617.

Mills, David. "The Dreams of Bunyan and Langland." *The Pilgrim's Progress: Critical and Historical Views.* Ed. Vincent Newey. Totowa: Barnes and Noble, 1980. 154–181.

Mitchell, Robert and Thurtle, Phillip, ed. "Introduction." *Data Made Flesh: Embodying Information.* New York: Routledge, 2004. 1–23.

Montag, Warren. *The Unthinkable Swift: The Spontaneous Philosophy of a Church of England Man.* London: Verso, 1994.

Moore, Benjamin. "Governing Discourses: Problems of Narrative Authority in *A Journal of the Plague Year.*" *The Eighteenth Century.* 33.2 (1992): 133–147.

Mueller, Judith C. "*A Tale of a Tub* and Early Prose." *The Cambridge Companion to Jonathan Swift.* Ed. Christopher Fox. Cambridge: Cambridge UP, 2003. 202–215.

Murray, George Evelyn. *The Post Office.* London: Putnam, 1927.

Newey, Vincent. "'With the eyes of my understanding': Bunyan, Experience, and Acts of Interpretation." *John Bunyan Conventicle and Parnassus: Tercentenary Essays.* Ed. N.H. Keeble. Oxford: Clarendon, 1988. 189–216.

Novak, Maximillian E. *Daniel Defoe: Master of Fictions, His Life and Ideas.* Oxford: Oxford UP, 2001.

———. "Defoe and the Disordered City." *Critical Essays on Daniel Defoe.* Ed. Roger D. Lund. New York: Hall, 1997. 218–235.

Nunberg, Geoffrey. "Farewell to the Information Age." *The Future of the Book.* Ed. Geoffrey Nunberg. Berkeley: U of California P, 1996. 103–138.

———. "Introduction." *The Future of the Book.* Ed. Geoffrey Nunberg. Berkeley: U of California P, 1996. 9–20.

Oakleaf, David. "Politics and History." *The Cambridge Companion to Jonathan Swift.* Ed. Christopher Fox. Cambridge: Cambridge UP, 2003. 31–47.

Ong, Walter. *Orality and Literacy: The Technologizing of the Word.* London: Routledge, 1982.

Paxman, David. "Oral and Literature Discourse in Aphra Behn's *Oroonoko.*" *Restoration: Studies in English Literary Culture, 1660–1700.* 18 (1994): 88–103.

Pearson, Jacqueline. "The History of *The History of the Nun.*" *Rereading Aphra Behn: History, Theory, and Criticism.* Ed. Heidi Hutner. Charlottesville: UP of Virginia, 1993. 234–252.

Poster, Mark. *The Mode of Information: Poststructuralism and Social Context.* Chicago: U of Chicago P, 1990.

Rabb, Melinda Alliker. "The Work of Women in the Age of Electronic Reproduction: The Canon, Early Modern Women Writers and the Postmodern

Reader." *A Companion to Early Modern Women's Writing.* Ed. Anita Pacheco. Oxford: Blackwell, 2002. 339–360.

Rawson, Claude. "Order and Cruelty: A Reading of Swift (with some comments on Pope and Johnson)." *Modern Critical Views: Jonathan Swift.* Ed. Harold Bloom. New York: Chelsea House, 1986. 83–106.

Reddick, Allen. "Avoiding Swift: Influence and the Body." *Locating Swift: Essays from Dublin on the 250th Anniversary of the Death of Jonathan Swift 1667–1745.* Ed. Aileen Douglas, Patrick Kelly, and Ian Campbell Ross. Dublin: Four Courts P, 1998. 150–166.

Reed, Walter L. *An Exemplary History of the Novel : The Quixotic Versus the Picaresque.* Chicago: U of Chicago P, 1981.

Richetti, John. *Daniel Defoe.* Boston: Hall, 1987.

Roberts, David. Introduction. *A Journal of the Plague Year.* By Daniel Defoe. Oxford: Oxford UP, 1990. vii–xxviii.

Robinson, Howard. *The British Post Office: A History.* Princeton: Princeton UP, 1948.

Rodowick, D.N. Introduction. *Mobile Citizens, Media States.* Spec. issue of *PMLA* 117.1 (2002): 13–23.

Ross, Angus and Woolley, David, ed. Introduction to *A Tale of a Tub and Other Works.* Ed. Angus Ross and David Woolley. Oxford: Oxford UP, 1984.

Ross, Deborah. *The Excellence of Falsehood: Romance, Realism, and Women's Contribution to the Novel.* Lexington: U of Kentucky P, 1991.

Rushworth, Nick. "'This Way of Printing Bits of Books': The Fiction of Incompletion in *A Tale of a Tub.*" *Representations of Swift.* Ed. Brian A. Connery. Newark: U of Delaware P, 2002. 41–56.

Sadler, Lynn Veach. *John Bunyan.* Boston: Twayne, 1979.

Schonhorn, Manuel. "Defoe's *Journal of the Plague Year:* Topography and Intention." *Review of English Studies.* 76 (1968): 387–402.

Sharrock, Roger. "'When at the first I took my Pen in hand': Bunyan and the Book." *John Bunyan Conventicle and Parnassus: Tercentenary Essays.* Ed. N.H. Keeble. Oxford: Clarendon, 1988. 71–90.

——. "Women and Children." 1966. *Bunyan's The Pilgrim's Progress: A Casebook.* Ed. Roger Sharrock. London: Macmillan, 1976. 174–186.

Shenk, David. *Data Smog: Surviving the Information Glut.* San Francisco: Harper-Collins, 1997.

Spencer, Jane. *Aphra Behn's Afterlife.* Oxford: Oxford UP, 2000.

Standage, Tom. *The Victorian Internet: The Remarkable Story of the Telegraph and the Nineteenth Century's On-line Pioneers.* New York: Berkley Books, 1998.

Starr, G.A. *Defoe & Casuistry.* Princeton: Princeton UP, 1971.

Stephanson, Raymond. "The Plague Narrative of Defoe and Camus." *Modern Language Quarterly.* 48.3 (1987): 224–241.

Stretton, Tim. "Women, Property and Law." *A Companion to Early Modern Women's Writing.* Ed. Anita Pacheco. Oxford: Blackwell, 2002. 40–57.

Suarez, Michael F. "Swift's Satire and Parody." *The Cambridge Companion to Jonathan Swift*. Ed. Christopher Fox. Cambridge: Cambridge UP, 2003. 112–127.

Swaim, Kathleen M. *Pilgrim's Progress, Puritan Progress: Discourses and Contexts*. Urbana, IL: U of Illinois P, 1993.

Swift, Jonathan. *Gulliver's Travels*. (1726) Ed. Robert Demaria, Jr. New York: Penguin, 2001.

——. *The Mechanical Operation of the Spirit*. (1704) Ed. Angus Ross and David Woolley. Oxford: Oxford UP, 1984.

——. *A Tale of a Tub and Other Works*. (1704) Ed. Angus Ross and David Woolley. Oxford: Oxford UP, 1984.

Terranova, Tiziana. *Network Culture: Politics for the Information Age*. London: Pluto P, 2004.

Todd, Janet. *The Secret Life of Aphra Behn*. New Brunswick: Rutgers UP, 1996.

——. "A Spectacular Death: History and Story in *The Widow Ranter*." *New Casebooks: Aphra Behn*. Ed. Janet Todd. New York: St. Martin's, 1999. 73–84.

Traugott, John. "Irony, Swift's Gift to the Reader in *A Tale of a Tub*." *Critical Approaches to Teaching Swift*. Ed. Peter J. Schakel. New York: AMS Press, 1992. 151–173.

von Sneidern, Maja-Lisa. *Savage Indignation: Colonial Discourse from Milton to Swift*. Newark: U of Delaware P, 2005.

Wainwright, V.L. "Lending to the Lord: Defoe's Rhetorical Design in *A Journal of the Plague Year*." *British Journal for Eighteenth-Century Studies*. 13.1 (1990): 59–72.

Walker, Claire. *Gender and Politics in Early Modern Europe: English Convents in France and the Low Countries*. New York: Palgrave Macmillan, 2003.

Warner, John. *Joyce's Grandfathers: Myth and History in Defoe, Smollett, Sterne, and Joyce*. Athens: U of Georgia P, 1993.

Watt, Ian. *The Rise of the Novel: Studies in Defoe, Richardson, and Fielding*. Berkeley: U of California P, 1957.

Wutz, Michael. "Introduction: Media—Models, Memories, and Metaphors." *Configurations*. 10.1 (2002): 1–10.

Wyrick, Laura. "Facing Up to the Other: Race and Ethics in Levinas and Behn." *The Eighteenth Century: Theory and Interpretation*. 40 (1999): 206–218.

Zipes, Jack. "The Instrumentalization of Fantasy: Fairy Tales and the Mass Media." *The Myths of Information: Technology and Postindustrial Culture*. Ed. Kathleen Woodward. Madison: Coda, 1980. 88–110.

Index